Green Roofs

A guide to their design and installation

Green Roofs

A guide to their design and installation

Angela Youngman

THE CROWOOD PRESS

First published in 2011 by
The Crowood Press Ltd
Ramsbury, Marlborough
Wiltshire SN8 2HR

www.crowood.com

British Library Cataloguing-in-Publication Data
A catalogue record for this book is available from the British Library.

ISBN 978 1 84797 296 5

Acknowledgements
Thanks are due to all the people and companies who helped in the research and providing illustrations for this book especially Bauder, Veg Tech, Angela Lambert of Enviromat, Simon Pöe of Alumasc, Bruce Hemstock of PWL Partnership and Jorg Breuning of Green Roof Services LLC. Thanks too go to Ian Youngman for his research help, Karis Youngman and Galen Youngman who helped so well with photographs. All photographs are by the author unless otherwise acknowledged.

Central front cover photo: GAP Photos/Jerry Harpur
Frontispiece: Derek St Romaine, Design: Stephen Hall/RHS Chelsea 2005

Typeset by Jean Cussons Typesetting, Diss, Norfolk

Printed and bound in India by Replika Press Pvt Ltd

CONTENTS

INTRODUCTION

Around the world, particularly in large cities, green roofs are appearing on everything from a small garden shed to a huge skyscraper. Some cities have even brought green roofs into their future planning. Along the way, the concept of a green roof has changed from just putting a few plants on top of a roof, to being part of the every-day use of a building. There are office blocks with large commercial greenhouses, catwalks for fash-ion shows, restaurants growing their own food and keeping bees, and even cruise liners and buses with a living roof.

The way green roofs are used has changed so much that it can be argued that living roof is a better name. More importantly, the green roof has changed from something that stands alone to being part of the overall greening of a building and landscape.

This is not a self-help manual, as most green roofs will need the involvement of architects, engineers, builders, plant specialists and safety experts. Green roofs are now a key element of the greening of buildings and cities. Anyone consid-ering the idea must regard it as part of the holistic attitude to environmentally friendly and energy efficient buildings, dealing with issues such as sustainability, heat islands and stormwater as well as biodiversity and aesthetics.

This book looks at the growth of green roofs in the past, present and future. While believing that green roofs are a good idea, it takes an analytical and independent, critical look at how the green roof movement is developing and changing.

Green roofs have a long history. For centuries people have been investigating ways of gardening on rooftops. Built in the seventh century BC, the Hanging Gardens of Babylon built by King Nebuchadnezzar and believed to be a series of terraces is the most famous example. But there are many others. Archaeologists have discovered roof gardens in the ruins of Roman Herculaneum buried under lava from Mount Vesuvius in AD79. Earth sheltered huts were common throughout the Viking world, while in Scandin-avia turf has continued to be used to cover roofs to the present day. It is still possible to find turf roofs in Norway that have existed since the eight-eenth century. During the Renaissance, the Palazzo Piccolomini at Pienza in Italy had a roof garden, as did the Benettoni Tower at Lucca. Sod houses with two feet thick walls and roofs made from strips of prairie sod (the tangled roots of buffalo grass and other native grasses) were found throughout the American mid-west during the nineteenth century. In the same century, roof gardens were built in Berlin and in London. The Home for Working Boys in Bishopsgate Street, City of London had a roof garden that contained large trees such as lime, fir, holly, chestnut and plane.

Yet it is only within the past fifty or so years that green roofs have really come to the forefront of everyone's attention. The reasons for this are simple. Firstly, green roofs are a concept that makes sense since roofs comprise most of the unused space in modern, overcrowded cities. In New York for instance, the available rooftop area is equal to twenty to thirty times the land area of Central Park. To take another example, in Greater London roofs cover over 24,000 hectares of land. This is twenty-eight times the size of Richmond Park, and equivalent to about 16 per cent of

OPPOSITE: A garden shed.
(Design: Cleve West; photo: Derek St Romaine)

A rural green-roofed home. (Photo: Karis Youngman)

London. Any attempt by planners and governments to make cities greener has to pay attention to the unused roof space – there is little available space at ground level.

Secondly, environmental concerns have become an increasing priority. Conventional roofs of concrete or tile have served as little more than waterproof ceilings for buildings. There is now increasing awareness that roofs can serve more than one function. Roofs offer considerable potential for dealing with climate problems such as stormwater surges and heat islands in urban areas, and can substantially reduce inner city temperatures. Roofs can also help increase biodiversity, providing habitats in what are otherwise concrete jungles. On a domestic level, ordinary houses benefit from reduced energy costs, as well as improving aesthetic qualities. Roofs can no longer be regarded in isolation – they are an essential part of the environment around us.

The modern trend towards the greening of roofs has developed from the use of sedum roofs in Scandinavia, Germany and Switzerland during the 1970s. In 1977, Friedensreich Hundertwasser built the famous Hundertwasserhaus – a low-income apartment block incorporating sedums on its roof. The publicity gained by that building and many others in central Europe focused the attention of consumers, businesses and local authorities on the green roof concept. It has now

LEFT: A roof that blends into the countryside. (Photo: Karis Youngman)

RIGHT: Stunning views over Singapore from one of the highest green roof parks in the world (Photo: Marina Bay Sands)

become a major industry throughout Europe, and is spreading worldwide with green roofs appearing on residential, commercial and public buildings in every continent from North America to China. Every country is showing an interest in green roofs, and investigating how green roofs can be used in their particular environments.

'When one creates green roofs, one doesn't need to fear the so-called paving of the landscape: the houses themselves become part of the landscape,' commented Friedensreich Hundertwasser, the Austrian artist and architect. It is an idea that is gaining considerable popularity in modern cities. Within concrete jungles, the green roofs are providing useful amenities in more ways than one – they are offering habitats for wildlife, reducing the amount of water going into sewers, acting as a cooling influence and providing a pleasant sight.

Most people tend to think of green roofs as being on top of multi-storey buildings or houses, clearly visible but usually out of reach. Yet they are more than this. Green roofs are found everywhere – on top of birdhouses, stables, pergolas, dog kennels, sheds and garages. They are found on top of motorways creating public parks for everyone to use; they are on tube stations, hotels, museums, and public buildings of all shapes and sizes. Green roofs have even been put on top of buses! Nor are roof gardens confined to simple sedum roofs – they can be public amenities, private gardens complete with trees and shrubs, or areas for growing food. In many cities and towns, if people want greenery or to create a garden, the only way to go is up. It is also becoming a way to grow food – on an industrial scale or an individual household basis. Although this is still in its infancy, food growing on roofs could be a way of reducing food miles substantially and enabling more people to enjoy fresh homegrown food.

The whole idea of a green roof has been transformed. It is now a concept that is available to everyone, from ordinary householders to big businesses with large budgets. A green roof can be as small or as large as the owner requires it to be, and in whatever format is preferred. It is possible to buy pre-packed modules, strips of sedum matting, tailor-made packages or to simply create a DIY version. Green roofs have become a multi-million pound industry with the end result benefitting the environment, improving landscaping and increasing property values.

1 WHAT IS A GREEN ROOF?

A green roof is a roof that is covered with some form of vegetation. This can be anything from turf to perennials, shrubs and vegetables. Green roofs can be installed on new buildings, and retrofitted onto existing ones. The only stipulation is that the building must be strong enough to hold the weight of the green roof with its heavy layer of soil and vegetation. There are several different types of green roof and clear distinctions have to be made between them.

NATURALLY OCCURRING GREEN ROOFS

A green roof can occur naturally over a long period of time. Nature will naturally cover any surface if it is left long enough. Soil-forming plants such as lichen, mosses and algae will develop on any roof, eventually creating conditions suitable for a wider range of plants. The rougher the surface, the easier it is for plants to colonize. Many concrete pillboxes dating from the Second World War have roofs that have been colonized by moss and lichen. Grass and wild plants such as *Sedum acre*, *Cardamine hirsuta*, *Senecio vulgaris* and *Sedum reflexum* can frequently be found growing in gutters. The seeds have reached the roofs as a result of natural dispersal by wind or birds. Recognizing this, there is an increasing trend for buildings to include brown roofs. These are roofs that are designed to become naturally-occurring green roofs. A substrata is the growing medium on the roof that enables the plants to colonize it. This is usually a mix of rubble and soil. Typical of this approach is Neatishead Village Hall, in Norfolk, which possesses both a sedum and a brown roof.

OPPOSITE: A living roof. (GAP Photos/Marcus Harpur; design Wendy Allen, Hadlow College with Westgate Joinery)

INTENSIVE GREEN ROOFS

Intensive green roofs are also known as roof gardens. These are flat roofs that possess a deep substrata of planting material which allows a wide range of plants to be grown such as trees, shrubs, flowers, vegetables and grasses. In general, such roofs reproduce traditional garden formats with lawns, flower beds, seating areas and planters. The Kensington Roof Gardens are a good example. Located on the sixth floor of the building, the

RIGHT: The Spanish Garden – An example of intensive roof design at the Kensington Roof Gardens. (Photo: Kensington Roof Gardens)

Intensive garden park style above the Castle Mall Shopping centre, Norwich.

Extensive green roof style using sedums on a residential building. (Photo: Karis Youngman)

gardens were originally opened in 1938, and were redesigned in 2008. They contain over seventy full-size trees, evergreen shrubs, roses and even a stream inhabited by ducks and flamingos. Intensive roof gardens are usually accessible to the general public or users of the building. Slightly simpler forms of intensive roof gardens can comprise lawns and ground-covering plants that are designed to be overlooked by other buildings, and have limited access.

These are the most expensive form of roof garden both to build and maintain. They require regular watering, weeding and general maintenance. Such gardens have to be easily accessible and roofs generally have to be substantially strengthened in order to bear the weight of soil, plants and regular human access.

EXTENSIVE ROOF GARDENS

Extensive roof gardens are designed to be self-sustaining and require very little maintenance. Covered in turf, wildflowers or sedum plants, these are the most common type of roof garden. It is the type most people immediately think of when the term green roof is mentioned. These are the roofs that are frequently appearing on top of commercial, industrial and public buildings as well as residential properties. Extensive green roofs are particularly suitable for small projects such as garden sheds, stables and dog kennels. Green roofs planted with turf, wildflowers and sedum require a much thinner layer of planting materials and can be used on flat or sloping roofs.

PLANT SPECIES

The number of green roofs worldwide has increased dramatically since the 1970s. Most of these new roofs are extensive roofs, planted with sedum, turf or wildflowers. Sedum is a very popular choice because it grows slowly reaching no more than 10cm (4in) in height, needs little watering and can withstand extremes of temperature. Sedum can cope with high winds, hot sun, drought, winter cold and wet. A succulent flowering plant, it comes in many different colours. Even when not flowering, it looks attractive as the stems are various shades of brown, yellow, green, and red. Sedum can be grown in a shallow layer of around 2cm (1in) of soil and has become the workhorse of the green roof movement. It is lightweight, and ideal for retrofits or new build projects. Having been used constantly since the

Sedums on a green roof.

Coloured sedums.

Wild flowers on a roof.

A clover roof.

The roof at Ralph's Place, which is slowly changing from a pure sedum to a native plant roof. (Photo: Galen Youngman)

Sedum and native prairie plants mix on the Target Center, Minneapolis, roof. (Design: Kestrel Design Group, Inspect and Leo A. Daly; Photo: Bergerson Photography)

Trees and mature shrubs grow well on this intensive roof garden.

1970s, it has been proved to work on roofs of any kind. Herbs and heathers have been used in Germany.

As the popularity of extensive green roofs has spread, so horticulturalists have been looking at alternative plant species, particularly plants which are native to the area. In the UK, species that are being recommended include *Armeria maritima*, basil thyme (*Clinopodium acinos*), Pasque flower (*Pulsatilla vulgaris*), Michaelmas daisies (*Aster Non-belgii*), Canadian golden rod (*Solidago canadensis*). On a wildflower roof, these varieties not only provide colour; they are also good for wildlife as they flower in late summer and autumn, and the plants provide valuable food sources for insects. Low growing bulbs such as crocuses are frequently added.

Clover is another popular plant for roofs. It creates all-year-round ground cover, with white flowers in summer. At the Eden Project, horse-shoe and kidney vetch have been seeded onto the roof with considerable success, providing food for butterflies and insects such as the rare, brown-banded bumble bee. Royal Horticultural Society scientist Tijana Blanusa reported at the Green Roof Congress in 2010, that *Stachys byzantina* (lambs' ears) could also be used on roofs. In trials, the leaf surface temperature of *Stachys byzantina* proved to be very low even through growth was slower due to minimal watering. 100 per cent ground coverage using *Stachys byzantina* was achieved within twenty-two days of the experiment starting. *Hedera* (ivy) also worked well.

Mosses, liverworts and lichens can be grown successfully on roofs. Although there has not been much research carried out on these plants, they naturally colonize roofs. While important for the environment, these plants do have less visual impact and do not look quite as attractive as sedums or other flowering plants. 'Ralph's Place' in Norfolk began as a sedum roof but is steadily being colonized by mosses and plants native to the locality.

Elsewhere in the world, a similar process is underway. Every country is investigating native plants to see what would grow on roofs. In North America considerable interest is being expressed concerning the use of native prairie plants on roofs, for example the Winnebago County Freedom Field green roof comprises 1,000ft^2 of native prairie plants. The Minnesota Target Center has over 113,000ft^2 of prairie plants such as *Sedum album* 'Coral Carpet', *Sedum sexangulare*, *Allium canadense*, *Liatris punctata*, *Lupinus perennis*, *Antennaria neglecta* and *Dalea purpurea*.

Over in Japan, research by Sendo, Kanechi and Inagaki (reported in the *Journal of the Japanese Society for Horticultural Science* 2010) investigated ten ornamental species to see how well they would grow in just 10cm (4in) of soil, leaf-mould and vermiculite substrate on a flat roof at Kobe, Japan. The planting undertaken by the researchers included *Evolvulus pilosus*, *Fragaria ananassa*, *Petunia hybrida* and *Thymus serpyllum*; all of which grew well and increased in coverage by more than 70 per cent.

Gardeners planning an intensive green roof can grow almost anything if the conditions are right. Most trees, shrubs, perennials and vegetables will grow quite successfully on a roof as long as they have enough soil and nutrients, and basic maintenance is undertaken on a regular basis. The key thing to bear in mind is that tall plants may need extra staking, particularly in windy areas. The wind and weather conditions found on top of roofs may reduce size and shape but as long as the roots are strong, and there is enough water, the plants will survive.

WHY ARE GREEN ROOFS BECOMING SO PREVALENT?

Since green roofs have been in existence in one form or another for so many centuries, the question has to be asked: why is there so much interest now? Why are green roofs in all their various formats becoming so prevalent?

Reasons are not hard to find. Green roofs do possess a lot of advantages and these are only now being fully recognized.

Above all, green roofs are increasingly seen as an answer to the problems of modern cities. More and more people are living in cities, and urban populations now surpass non-urban populations worldwide. The United Nations has indicated that it expects the percentage of the world population living in urban areas to grow from 50 per cent to 70 per cent by 2050. This will mean that the total number living in urban areas then will be close to the entire world population at the start of the twenty-first century. This poses an immediate climatic problem.

Most cities have limited amounts of green vegetation at ground level. Buildings are placed close together. Limited land availability means high land costs. Buildings are getting higher and higher in order to accommodate as many people as possible in a small area. Urban surfaces conventionally use dark materials such as concrete, cement, tarmac and tiles. These store up more heat than natural surfaces like wood and grass. As a result, the urban man-made surfaces take up heat during the day and then release it much more slowly at night. This helps keep the temperatures high, making cities very hot at night during the summer. Added to this is the heat created by motor vehicles and air conditioning; all of which combine to create urban heat islands experiencing much higher heat levels than in rural areas. To make matters worse, the high temperatures cause a decrease in air quality. Pollution from vehicles, homes, offices and factories is magnified when chemicals in the air react with heat and sunlight creating poor ozone quality often referred to as smog. This can irritate people's eyes, aggravate asthma and cause permanent lung damage.

Combined with this problem of urban heat islands, energy prices are rising and winters are getting colder as a result of climate change. Rooftops – which have been a hitherto unused resource offering a lot of space – are seen as a key way of helping deal with the situation. Traditionally roofs have been made of tiles, or slabs of concrete in the cities. Planners are seeking to encourage the use of lighter coloured, replacement materials that are more environmentally friendly – white, blue or green roofs that can decrease temperature levels.

White Roofs

White roofs (also known as cool roofs) are regarded as a quick answer to heat problems. This involves spraying rooftops with a white, rubbery layer that reflects the sun's rays back into the sky. Just as light-coloured clothes are more comfortable than dark ones on a hot day, so white roofs can make an immediate difference. This method is proving very popular in cities like New York, USA and Melbourne (Australia) as it is cheap, immediately lowers the energy costs of a building and has an overall effect on decreasing the urban heat island effect. These roofs can be particularly useful in areas where there are consistent high temperatures.

The disadvantage is that they do not deal with stormwater problems, or help encourage biodiversity. In addition, they are not always pleasant to see as they can get dirty quite quickly, thus requiring regular maintenance to stay effective. Little research has been conducted on the longevity of the white membranes.

Blue Roofs

Blue roofs utilize captured stormwater for cooling and insulation. These are a very new idea, and research is still underway on how they work and how effective blue roofs are in practice.

GREEN ROOFS

These are regarded as the most aesthetically pleasing as well as being environmentally friendly. They are extremely popular because they possess the greatest range of environmental benefits such as reducing energy costs, decreasing the temperatures of urban heat islands and helping deal with stormwater. In addition they encourage biodiversity within a built-up environment. Green roofs are also visually attractive and can blend into a landscape, often making planning permission easier to obtain. They gain environmental points wherever they are built. In Canada for example, green roofs can increase a building's environmental rating when linked into other sustainable building elements such as:

- landscape design that reduces urban heat islands
- storm-water management
- water-efficient landscaping
- innovative waste water technologies
- reduced site disturbance
- protect or restore open spaces.

It is recognition of the sheer number of advantages and benefits possessed by green roofs that has encouraged their popularity worldwide. Energy savings are substantial. The Tokyo based Organization for Landscape and Urban Greenery Technology development estimated in 2003 that if only half the roofs in Tokyo were green, a reduction of 0.84° C would be experienced in summer daytime temperatures. This would immediately save 110 million Yen in air-conditioning costs.

THE ADVANTAGES OF GREEN ROOFS

Insulation

Green roofs provide insulation. The vegetation on green roofs reflects solar heat away from the roof membrane. It reduces the amount of heat leaving a building in winter. The fuel cost savings have been estimated at 2 litres of fuel oil per square metre. In general, exact savings on energy heating and cooling costs depend on the size of the building, the climate and type of green roof that has been installed.

In the summer, a green roof provides shade from strong sunlight, helping keep buildings cooler inside. This reduces the need for air conditioning and thus reduces CO2 emissions. The United States Laboratories Public Health Building in Salt Lake City noted that as soon as a green roof was installed on the building, the interior temperature was reduced to 70°F even when the outside temperature was reaching 110°F.

Preliminary results of a green roof trial carried out by the University of Melbourne in 2009 revealed that green roofs reduced electricity requirements for air conditioning by 48 per cent during the summer. In the winter, heating requirements were reduced by 13 per cent. Dr Nicolas Williams of the University of Melbourne indicated that although both white and green roofs were successful in shielding buildings from solar radiation, green roofs were more successful since the vegetation helped cool the overall environment by evaporating water and filtering stormwater, thus reducing the amount which carried pollutants into rivers.

These findings are matched by research carried out at the Centre for Climate Systems Research, Columbia University in the USA. Columbia University researchers have been putting research meteorological stations on a variety of green roofs within New York City. Plants were seen to be thriving in the harsh environment of tower block roofs and researchers discovered that the green roof had almost eliminated the rooftop as an urban heat source. The absence of extreme temperature cycles helps to prove why green roofs are expected to outlast traditional membranes by two or more times, since the accompanying thermal expansions and contractions are greatly reduced.

Using a Micro Axess Simulation model, researchers at Environment Canada discovered that a typical one-storey building with a grass roof and 10cm (4in) of growing medium would result in a 25 per cent reduction in summer cooling needs. While experiments in Ottawa, Canada indicated that a 15cm (6in) extensive green roof reduced heat gains by 95 per cent and heat losses by 26 per cent compared to a standard roof.

Energy savings throughout a city can be substantially reduced as a result of greening rooftops. Green roofs reduce the amount of air conditioning required, thus ensuring that smaller amounts of equipment would be needed to provide air conditioning. This in turn provides savings on capital equipment and long term investment as well as energy costs. In 1999, the City of Chicago estimated that greening city rooftops would result in energy savings of at least $100m that could be saved annually due to decreased demand for air conditioning.

The extent to which a green roof provides winter insulation as opposed to summer cooling does depend greatly on the location and climate. Within the UK and other northern countries, winter insulation is not as big a benefit simply because the roof becomes saturated with cold water. In the summer it does have a cooling effect.

Urban Heat Islands

Green roofs can decrease the overall temperature of cities making them pleasanter to live and work in during the summer period. Traditional dark roofs absorb sunlight and radiate heat into the atmosphere. The solar heat trapped in the fabric of buildings, together with heat trapped in busy streets, creates urban heat islands where there is minimal cooling from breezes or vegetation. Air conditioners move hot air from inside buildings into the streets. A flat gravel roof can be up to 21°C hotter than a green roof.

In climate science, the reflectivity of a surface is described as an 'albedo'. Dark materials such as concrete and tiles have a low albedo – just 5 per cent. The remaining 95 per cent of solar radiation experienced by a dark roof is absorbed by the roof and turned into heat energy, releasing it during the night. White roofs have albedos of around 75 to 80 per cent, leaving only 20 to 25 per cent of heat energy to be absorbed by the roof. Green roofs work differently – the plants turn the sun-

The difference a green roof makes to an urban area. (Design: Kestrel Design Group, Inspect and Leo A. Daly; photo: Bergerson Photography)

light into water vapour. The vegetation on a green roof acts as a coolant, reducing the amount of heat being absorbed by the building. The greater the number of green roofs within an area, the greater the overall decrease in temperatures within the urban area as a whole. Less heat is being released at night from buildings, thus making the area cooler.

Studies have shown that green roofs can lower heat island temperatures by at least 3°C, if not more.

Rainwater

A vegetative green roof reduces the amount of rainwater leaving a roof. The vegetation automatically retains some of the water, as does the planting material underneath. Research has shown that rainwater is reduced by at least 50 per cent, sometimes much higher, for example the Steinhart Aquarium/Morrison Planetarium green roof in San Francisco has seen a 90 per cent reduction in stormwater run-off since the roof was fitted.

At least 15 per cent to 20 per cent of stormwater rainwater is actually retained on the roof for at least two months before draining away. This decreases the risk of flooding as a result of stormwater surges after periods of heavy rainfall. Instead the water drains away much more slowly over a period of time from a green roof. Many owners of green roofs say that rain does not actually start running off a roof for at least an hour after it starts raining.

The exact reduction levels in stormwater run-off vary from country to country. Research findings are varying from 20 to 100 per cent depending on where the roof is installed. Within the UK, it is generally between 35 to 50 per cent. Research carried out at Sheffield University indicated that of thirty rainfall periods in which over 5mm of rain fell, green roofs did provide a significant benefit, reducing the amount of stormwater run-off even when the roof was saturated. The type of substrate can make a difference as it can vary between plus or minus 28 per cent.

A green roof is increasingly being seen as an integral part of a wider rainwater harvesting project. Water is a scarce resource, particularly during summer periods. Gardeners have traditionally channelled water from drainpipes leading from the roof into water butts. This is now being expanded into developing storage tanks holding larger quantities of water that can be used for many uses such as watering the garden, flushing toilets or doing the laundry. Rainwater harvesting systems can replace up to 50 per cent of household water and 80 per cent of the water used in commercial buildings according to the UK Rainwater Harvesting Association. Such a link between a green roof and rainwater harvesting can be seen at the Adnams Brewery Distribution Centre, Southwold. The 0.6 acre sedum roof provides a vast rainwater catchment which, combined with a sustainable urban drainage system, enables the company to harvest rainwater from the roof and other surface areas. On a much smaller scale, the Eco-Shed in Potter Heigham has been designed to capture all surplus rainwater into underground tanks which can be accessed via pumps leading to water butts.

Anti-Pollutant

Green roofs act as a useful filter of polluting chemicals. The plants and soil filter the rain as it passes through the roof to the drainage mats. This acts as a buffer against acid rain by removing nitrates and other contaminated materials. In 1993, the London Ecology Unit publication entitled *Building Green – a guide to using plants on roofs, walls and pavements* stated that 95 per cent of heavy metals are removed from water by green roofs; and that nitrogen levels were also reduced. These findings were echoed by research carried out by Auckland Regional Council in 2003 where researchers discovered that green roofs could remove 75 per cent of suspended solids. During the monitoring period of the research, nitrogen levels from the green roof varied between 10mg and 80mg per square metre compared to nitrogen discharges from conventional roofs of 265mg per square metre. Phosphate levels decreased to between 75m and 100mg per square metre compared to 145mg per square from a conventional roof.

A green roof absorbs most air pollutants, heavy metals and dust as well as greenhouse gases like carbon dioxide. In addition, plants utilize excess carbon dioxide to provide oxygen. This can make a tremendous improvement in the air quality in towns particularly during the summer when ozone levels can be high.

Biodiversity

As urban areas expand, the available green space within its boundaries shrinks. In London, buildings are estimated to cover 16 per cent of the city, about 24,000 hectares of land. As open space within cities and towns is reduced, so the biodiversity of the wildlife and fauna is substantially reduced. It becomes harder for birds and invertebrates to find suitable food or nesting areas. Green roofs have become a key element in dealing with the problem as the vegetation on the roof can provide oases of greenery. Two different approaches can be used to encourage biodiversity:

- recreating threatened vegetation and habitats
- supporting specific species or groups of species as it is important to create the correct type of conditions that will enable populations to establish themselves.

Log piles to encourage biodiversity.

The use of local and native plant species together with relevant substrates that reflect the local environment will increase the overall biodiversity value of a green roof.

In the UK, green roofs are often used as replacements for habitats lost during urban regeneration projects especially on brown field sites, which were previously used for industrial or commercial purposes and may have become contaminated. The vegetation on green roofs can provide a valuable link in green space networks throughout an urban area. Often the green roofs may be the only available green space for some distance.

Research by English Nature has shown that green roofs can provide new habitats, as well as creating new links across existing habitats encouraging the movement and dispersal of wildlife. English Nature have estimated that if green roofs are incorporated into redevelopment and refurbishment projects, this could result in a large proportion of this space being opened up to wildlife. Nesting sites can be provided by green roofs for a wide range of birds such as pigeons, house sparrows, skylarks, owls, robins, wagtails, tits, house martins, swallows, and fly catchers. Bats, too, can be attracted to green roofs.

Swiss research by Brenneisen has shown that the height of the building makes no difference to birds. This means that green roofs could easily be used to provide good nesting and feeding areas for declining species such as house sparrows as well as rare species like black redstarts that like brown field sites. Green roofs are increasingly included in biodiversity action plans within urban areas. Features such as log piles, bird boxes, bird feeding stations or pipes to provide protection for the chicks of ground nesting birds can be easily incorporated into a green roof.

It is not only birds that are attracted to green roofs. Numerous varieties of insects such as bees, wasps, beetles, spiders, butterflies and moths can be found on a green roof. A study carried out in 2007 at the University of Sheffield, focusing on bumblebees, discovered that no less than six different bee species were regularly visiting two green roofs. The species found were the common carder bumblebee, red-tailed bumblebee, early nesting bumblebee, buff-tailed bumblebee, white-tailed bumblebee and the garden bumble-

Honey bee on a green roof. (Photo: Jorg Breuning/Green Roof Service LLG)

bee. The wildflower roof attracted more bees than the sedum roof.

Biodiversity is becoming ever more important in the installation of green roofs. In Sheffield, the local authority has introduced a Habitat Action Plan designed to increase the biodiversity value of all new green roofs in the city by setting specific targets, actions and guidance emphasizing local priority habitats and species. It includes a practical scoring system to be used as a guide for developers, planners, architects and BREEAM (BRE Group Environmental Assessment) ecologists when considering the potential biodiversity value of green roofs.

Education

Within urban areas, a green roof can provide a site for environmental education facilities that may be lacking at ground level. Children can be taught about conservation and biodiversity by studying the number of birds and insects that use the roof. For some children, this may be their only opportunity to see wildlife, and see the complex nature of the natural world in action.

With increasing emphasis being placed on teaching children how to grow vegetables, many inner city schools face the problem of where this can be done. Gardening on the roof is becoming more common. At Sharrow School in Sheffield, the two aims of providing environmental educational facilities and teaching gardening were combined when the school installed green roofs.

Aesthetics

Green roofs are very aesthetically pleasing. A green roof of any kind looks much better than a plain grey or black surface, adding interest to all the buildings that overlook it. By providing a green roof, it creates a positive image for a building as well as the organization that owns it. The positive image is further reinforced by the fact that the materials used to construct a green roof are environmentally friendly. The growing medium often includes recycled materials such as crushed brick and concrete while membranes and drainage mats are manufactured from recycled plastic.

There is an added aesthetic benefit in that creating access to an open space on the roof can increase the value of a property, especially in towns and cities. People are prepared to pay a premium for such space, particularly if good views are also available.

Green roofs can provide useful amenity space within cities where there may be little similar space. It can be used for recreational purposes. Green roofs have been used to provide golf courses, football pitches, inner city farms and hospital gardens. There are many instances of green roofs being turned into public parks. The most well known of these is in Linz, Germany where the Bindermichl Motorway tunnel running through the centre of the city has been turned into a green roof 8.13 hectare park. In Amsterdam, the Museumplein is a popular recreational destination for city dwellers. Likewise in Norwich, UK, the Castle Mall shopping centre has a green roof, which has become a popular public park where children play and people socialize. It also provides vehicular access to the adjacent medieval castle. Most people would not even realize that they were walking on the roof of a shopping centre when going through the park.

Noise Pollution

The vegetative layer absorbs noise. Both soil and plants help to insulate the interior of a building against noise from outside, or internal noise escaping to the outside. Sound waves produced by machinery, traffic, discotheques, industrial sites or aeroplanes can be absorbed, reflected or deflected by a green roof. Research has shown that the substrates used on green roofs deal with lower sound frequencies, while plants block higher frequencies. A green roof with a 12cm (4.5in) substrate layer can reduce noise levels by 40 decibels, while a 20cm (8in) substrate layer can reduce noise levels by 46–50 decibels.

A green roof can also reduce the amount of electromagnetic waves entering a building.

Lifespan

The creation of a green roof on top of a building immediately increases the life span of the roof itself. It has been estimated that the roof life is at least doubled. Covering a roof with a green roof can extend the life expectancy of a roof from thirty to sixty years.

A green roof can open up extra living space. (Photo: Ulrik Reeh, Veg Tech)

Castle Mall Gardens, Norwich.

There is less need for repairs over the lifespan of the roof. This is because the soil and vegetation protects the roof from sunlight and ultra violet radiation as well as temperature fluctuations that can cause traditional roofing materials to degrade. A green roof also reduces the costs of drainage, heating and air conditioning.

On any roof, it is the membranes that cover it that are most liable to deteriorate over time. Research has been shown that dark materials undergo major temperature swings throughout the day, due to variations in day and night temperatures. These swings cause expansion and contractions in the surface, which ultimately lead to a deterioration in the condition of the roof. Green roofs undergo very low temperature swings, thus extending the lifespan of the membrane, which is itself further protected by vegetation from the rays of the sun.

On a commercial basis, green roofs are often seen as a long-term investment. It is a way of increasing a building's future value by avoiding possible future legislative demands and reducing flood risks.

Although there have been suggestions that green roofs are regarded as having a higher fire risk than conventional roof materials; there have been no major incidents of fire in Germany or Switzerland where thousands of metres of green roofs have been installed since the 1970s. In fact, in Germany fire insurance premiums are actually lower on buildings possessing green roofs. Gravel fire breaks are required on green roofs and the amount of combustible materials has to be kept to a minimum.

Further benefits are likely to appear as more and more research is undertaken into green roof technology. The use of roofs as a means of growing food is still in its infancy, but already some organizations have reported significant savings. The Fairmount Waterfront Hotel in Vancouver grows herbs, flowers and vegetables on its roof reducing its food budget by $30,000 a year. Growing food on a roof enables food miles to be substantially reduced and further utilizes hitherto unused space within a city where there is limited space for allotments.

A particularly interesting development has been the discovery that green roofs and solar energy work extremely well together. Solar panels have been shown to work more efficiently when installed on a green roof, simply because the vegetation reduces the fluctuation of temperatures and maintains a more efficient micro-climate around the panels.

GREEN ROOFS VERSUS WHITE ROOFS

Green roofs are recognized to have much greater benefits than white roofs. Although white roofs are initially cheaper, they tend to have a shorter lifespan.

In 2008, a study of green and white roofs on the Con Edison Training and Conference Centre, Long Island, New York set out to compare the environmental benefits. It installed 250,000ft^2 of white roofing plus a quarter acre of green roof.

The conclusions made interesting reading. The survey discovered that both types of roofs worked equally well in dealing with the heat island effect. The green roof worked well keeping heat in the building during winter, and reducing the amount of heat entering the building during summer. In fact, the summer heat was reduced by 84 per cent, and winter heat losses were reduced by 67 per cent. There was less need for heating or air conditioning, and the green roof was much more energy efficient, saving approximately $400 per year in heating costs and $250 a year in cooling costs.

By comparison, the white roof only reduced summer heat levels by 67 per cent. Its energy saving was limited to reduced air conditioning costs – $200 a year.

By far the biggest problem of white roofs is the potential decreasing level of reflectivity that can occur. A white roof darkens and loses its reflectivity over time; this makes it less effective in dealing with heat, unless it is very regularly cleaned and maintained.

Costs

Installing a green roof is more expensive than a roof comprising traditional materials. The actual construction of a building may need to be strengthened as a green roof does weigh substantially more than a conventional one. The actual cost depends very much on specification and size of roof. Inevitably, an intensive green roof complete with shrubs and trees will be much more expensive than an extensive sedum or wildflower version.

However, the ultimate savings in terms of energy reduction, stormwater run-off and water harvesting can outweigh the construction costs. A research study carried out in Birmingham estimated that one plot with a green roof could make a saving of £173,000 for reductions in surface water costs. Taking into account a conservative figure of £53,000 for structural alterations, researchers estimated that overall cost savings could be around £120,000.

The occupiers of a building with a green roof will obviously experience a long term gain in reduced costs throughout the life of the building and these will be experienced each year. For larger projects, the local community, planning authorities and environmental organizations also gain substantially from benefits relating to reduced stormwater levels, that is, a reduced risk of flooding, reduced amounts of CO_2 in the climate, reduced heat island effects and reduced energy consumption.

A green roof is more than just a layer of planting material and plants. It is built up in layers and can add hundreds of pounds in weight to the roof. Having first ensured that the roof is strong enough to hold the weight of the green roof, the key ingredients are a waterproof membrane, drainage substrates, planting material and then the vegetation. Edging restraints will be required around a pitched roof to ensure that material does not slide down onto the ground below.

Choosing materials depends on personal taste, as well as any building restrictions that may be enforced. Considerable research is being undertaken into improving materials throughout the

Hillside setting for a green roof, showing how it blends into a rural environment. (Photo: Karis Youngman)

industry. Substrate material is formed from a variety of materials such as aggregates, construction waste, crushed brick, limestone and shale. To be effective, it needs a good balance of inorganic and organic matter. European guidelines recommend a minimum of 70 per cent inorganic matter to 30 per cent organic matter on intensive roofs. Extensive roofs can take a higher inorganic (90 per cent) to organic (10 per cent) level. A minimum substrate of 75mm (3in) is recommended to ensure there is sufficient water retention for the long-term survival of the green roof. Research by the Royal Horticultural Society, funded by the Waste and Resources Action Programme, has indicated that the amount of green compost within the planting substrate could be increased. The compost tested contained food and green waste plus Biochar charcoal. This combination was proved to increase the amount of nutrients held in the substrate. Biochar is a fine-grained, porous material that is high in carbon and ideal for use as a soil conditioner as it enhances plant growth and enables the soil to retain nutrients.

In general, natural and local substrate material is much more suitable for encouraging biodiversity. This is now being taken into account by some planning authorities dealing with large scale developments; for example in Basel there is a policy requiring all new development sites to conserve local topsoil for use on the green roofs in the locality.

LEGISLATION

Official policy on green roofs varies from country to country, and city to city within a country, reflecting the maturity of the industry within a particular area.

Green roofs are subject to the same laws and building regulations as any other roof. There is no known specific regulation on green roofs. But, in most countries the official legislation on buildings is backed up by a host of codes of practice on materials, methods and safety. Although codes of practice have no legal force as such, courts take these into account on any legal case. So owners and constructors of green roofs should take these seriously.

In the UK, to encourage the usage of green roofs, the Green Roof Centre is preparing a UK code of Best Practice for the design and installation of green roofs. The aim is to develop a code that will ensure the quality of design and installation, as well as providing assistance in achieving planning conditions.

Although some UK cities have indicated an

interest in encouraging green roofs, the only city so far to include green roofs within official planning policy is London. The London Plan of 2008 included the first policy in Britain focusing specifically on green roofs. It stated that all major developments should include green roofs within their design and that smaller green-roof projects should be encouraged by all thirty-two London Boroughs. This policy was continued in the Climate Change Adaptation Strategy adopted by Mayor Boris Johnson in 2010. Under the strategy, it proposed that all major developments within London's central zone (the city of London, most of Westminster, the inner parts of Camden, Islington, Hackney, Tower Hamlets, Southwark, Lambeth, Kensington and Chelsea) would be required to include a green roof. If this was not feasible, a cool white roof should be used.

Many local authorities are including green roofs within their desired plans for developments. New buildings in Sheffield from 2011 onwards will be required to include an 80 per cent green roof on any building of over 1,000m^2 or a development of more than ten dwellings. The London Borough of Lewisham states in its policy document *A Natural Renaissance for Lewisham* (2006–2011) that it aims to promote green roofs in all new developments of any kind across the borough. In the countryside, green roofs will often make a new house much more acceptable, particularly in sensitive areas, because it blends into the environment.

It is important to check locally whether planning permission is required for a green roof, especially on a permanent structure like an office or garage.

Outside of the UK, several cities have an official policy to encourage green roofs, for example Toronto and Chicago. As Green Roofs for Healthy Cities Chairman Jeffrey L. Bruce points out 'we are definitely seeing the emergence of more public policies and direct investment that support the implementation of green roof infrastructure due to its many public benefits, such as stormwater management, air quality improvement and reducing the urban heat island effect.'

Flood and stormwater legislation is becoming more of an issue worldwide and where this is introduced, green roofs are becoming an essential part of the measures required. It can be a major reason why businesses introduce green roofs both for new build and retrofits; and will open up a large market.

PROBLEMS

As with any roof or structure, problems can occur. The key problem areas are:

Poor installation

If the contractors, or whoever is installing the roof, make mistakes or cut corners when undertaking the construction, there may be long-term leaks or other damage.

Poor maintenance

Low maintenance does not mean that no maintenance is necessary. People often forget this. A green roof will require some care and attention each year. If left alone, the roots will deteriorate with unwanted, deep-rooted plants appearing, which if left could damage the various membranes. Roofs may need watering during very dry periods. If gutters and drains become blocked by vegetation or growing medium, it can cause problems.

Access

If access to the roof is difficult, it will be hard to maintain it.

Above all everything on the roof needs to be secure, to ensure that materials do not fall off. Philippine Association of Landscape Artists, Dicky Altavas criticized a roof garden on a commercial building which was designed by consultants unfamiliar with the climate in the Philippines. According to Altavas, the floor material used for the garden is an indoor surface and becomes slippery when it rains. There is no drainage, and the palm trees are not stable.

2 GREEN ROOFS IN USE – CONSUMER

There has long been a tradition of using vegetation to cover house roofs. Earth-sheltered structures have been used for centuries, particularly in Scandinavia and in the United States. Sod houses were the main means of providing quick, easy houses among the pioneers who set out to build homes during the opening of the western half of America in the nineteenth century. Writing in *The Sod House*, Cass G. Barns states that:

> the roof was the most difficult thing to provide and most of the sod house homesteaders made the roof of crooked limbs, brush, coarse prairie hay and a thick covering of sod and dirt. To hold up such a load, a forked tree was planted in each end of the house and a ridge pole log placed from one gable to the other resting in the forks. From the ridge pole to the walls, poles and limbs were laid.

Elsewhere, earth houses are still being built. These are usually built into the sides of cliffs or quarries with the green roof designed to increase insulation and allow it to blend into the landscape. In Cumbria, a house and veterinary surgery were built in 2002 into the side of an old quarry. Within a very short time grass began to grow on the roofs and the buildings merged back into the landscape. More recent buildings, such the Sedum House in North Norfolk, have installed sedum roofs as these can be easier to maintain.

Green roofs are being used on every possible form of domestic building – from stables to house roofs, seating areas, pergolas, kennels, bee hives, sheds, rabbit hutches, extensions, garages and garden buildings such as home offices. Within urban areas, green roofs are often regarded as a good way of gaining planning permission. It can certainly decrease the chance of neighbours objecting to a building such as a garden room even if it is overlooked by neighbouring houses. A green roof is much less intrusive. Neighbours are happier to see a stretch of green than an area of concrete, timber or tiles. In rural areas, the ability

Beehive with green roof.

OPPOSITE: Sedums on the roof of the garden pavilion at Lucy Redman's School of Garden Design. (Photo: GAP Photos/Zara Napier)

TOP: A garden building with a sedum roof.

LEFT: Sedum matting covering a compost bin.

River Quarter developments in Sunderland. (Photo: Alumasc)

of a green roof to blend into the landscape is very popular.

Environmental concerns and aesthetic qualities tend to dominate domestic green roofs of any size. Recognition of insulation and drainage qualities have been much slower to be made. If anything, the benefits of stormwater run-off have been the least recognized by most people.

There are an increasing number of large-scale housing developments automatically incorporating green roofs. This is true of both new build and refurbishment properties. Government funding and housing grants play a major part in ensuring the success of these schemes.

Typical of the new build projects is the £10 million mixed-use development by Gentoo Ventures in Sunderland. The scheme comprises a mix of commercial and residential development across eleven floors. There are fifty-three apartments, a residents' car park, bowling emporium and café bar. The roof garden was installed directly over the car park. To take another example, the Barking Riverside Development in East London will incorporate green roofs on 40 per cent of the 11,000 homes being built on the site.

There are signs that developers are beginning to consider green roofs as part of the wider, energy-efficient home concept. In Westbourne, Chichester a group of eco-friendly bungalows incorporating green roofs along with solar panels and energy-saving heating have been built for letting by the local council. The houses gained a

Green roofs at Academy Central Apartments. (Photo: Taylor Wimpey)

higher than normal Social Housing Grant from the Homes and Communities Agency (HCA) due to the energy efficiency of the design. In London, Taylor Wimpey are building 936 houses and apartments on the former site of the University of East London. Known as 'The Academy', the aim is for 20 per cent of all energy use within the development to come from renewable sources. All thirteen apartment buildings will have either a green sedum or a brown roof which will provide a 40 per cent increase in insulation to the buildings.

Retrofitting green roofs on existing housing developments is more complex, but is becoming more common. The Ethelred Estate, Kennington in the London Borough of Lambeth is the UK's largest green-roof renewal project. The complex contains ten separate buildings with a total of 253 apartments. A total of 4,000m^2 of sedum matting has been installed over the ten buildings. The roof has been designed to improve the view from surrounding tower blocks; as well as improving insulation and reducing noise from aircraft.

A smaller retrofit project was undertaken at Hornton Court, Kensington in London. The red brick Edwardian building was converted into luxury apartments, and roof terraces were added to the front of the building. The building had originally been designed with ornate gardens but these had been removed and replaced with paving. The refurbishment aimed to provide a green roof that would echo the original gardens. A Bauder Intensive green roof system was installed over the existing asphalt, and then planting beds were added.

Community involvement can be a strong motivator for the development of a green roo

Refurbished intensive roof garden at Hornton Court, Kensington, London. (Photo: Bauder)

project, particularly one which has more than one use. Such roofs tend to be intensive schemes with good public access. Dalston Roof Park in London is inspired by the style of traditional English country gardens. Initiated by Natasha Yildiz and the charity, Boot Strap Company; the garden is on the roof of the Print House in Ashwin Street, Dalston. A pop-up community space was created which could be enjoyed throughout the summer and act as a prototype for ways in which green spaces can pop up anywhere at relatively little cost. The garden has a white picket fence, a shed, carefully mown lawn and border flowers. During the summer, the garden is used by a local children's literacy scheme while at night there is a programme of evening events such as dance, poetry readings and film projections. The scheme is funded by a one time membership fee of £5.

In Manchester, green roofs form part of a major environmental regeneration project known as Little Green Roofs. It attempts to transform the roofs of small, uninhabited communal buildings and structures such as sheds, bike shelters and storage containers into havens for wildlife. All the roofs have to be part of a community initiative with local organizations such as residential associations becoming involved. Bren Fawcett from NEPHRA residential association in New Moston comments that it is projects like this which create community pride and stop anti-social behaviour.

> The kids see how beautiful everything including the roof, looks and they leave it alone because they respect the time and effort we have put in and they want to keep it that way. People are intrigued and it benefits everyone. It brought

Transforming a water tank into a green roof in Manchester. (Photo: Red Rose Forest/Outerspace Landscapes)

together different people including local volunteers, day centre staff, service users and Red Rose Forest staff. It was great fun and helped build friendships, confidence and community spirit.

Shaw's Cottage in the London Borough of Lewisham is an interesting domestic example of green roof development within an urban area. The two-storey, timber-framed house was built with a green roof in the late 1990s. The changes in planting that have taken place during two decades show how a green roof can mature and adapt to its circumstances. The roof was designed with a variety of substrates, with gravel and soil on flat areas while chalk, rubble and garden soil were used on pitched sections. The roof was partly covered with lawn grass and partly left to colonize naturally. *Sedum acre* and *Sedum reflexum* were added to the gravel area to speed up the process.

By 2001, the areas left to colonize naturally had joined together. Vegetation on all surfaces was fully covered. The main plant species present were *Geranium molle* (70 per cent cover) and *Tortula muralis* (40 per cent) on chalk rubble, while on the gravel/soil mix *Tortula muralis* dominated with around 70 per cent coverage, followed by *Sedum reflexum* at 40 per cent . There have been reports that a fox often lies up on the roof, while wasps have nested in the lawn areas. The roof has clearly aided biodiversity in the area, and played a valuable role in replacing lost habitats.

Recognizing the opportunities presented by green roofs, architects are beginning to look at ways of using them in innovative ways. In France, the Wave House created by Patrick Nadeau takes the form of a wooden, hull-like structure entirely covered by vegetation. Earth and plants protect against summer heat and winter cold. The green roof blends seamlessly into green walls and comes down to a podium upon which the house is built.

Over in Germany, the Hansa-Kolleg housing development in Hamburg uses an underground garage roof area between the building complexes to provide private gardens, play areas and leisure areas for residents. A striped theme was adopted so as to fit in with the design of the buildings. Ventilation shafts for the garages were hidden among hedgerows dividing private gardens from the public areas. While in Denmark, the Mountain Dwellings housing complex in Copenhagen has an unusual, mountain style design. All the apartments in the eleven-storey block have roof gardens facing the sun, with car parking placed on the tenth floor. The result is a building in which gardens cascade down the apartment block to resemble a gentle hillside.

Smaller DIY schemes and projects initiated on individual homes are very common. In Potter Heigham, Norfolk; an Eco-Shed shaped like a grand piano has been built which incorporates a green roof planted with sedums, wild flowers, gras

The sedum roof on a new-build Barratt Green House. (Photo: Bauder)

and clover. Individually designed family homes often incorporate a green roof – Ralph's Place and the Sedum House both in Norfolk are good examples of this. Individualistic projects such as the Barratt Green House incorporate green roofs as part of the overall emphasis on sustainability.

Within the UK, green roofs will undoubtedly benefit from the Coalition Government's Green Deal which is due to become law in 2012. The UK housing stock is responsible for around one quarter of all UK carbon emissions, but householders are reluctant to take action because of high up-front costs. The Green Deal is a way of providing support for energy efficiency measures to householders without having to meet those initial costs. It is a radical way of making energy efficiency available to everyone, whether people own or rent their property. Work to upgrade properties will be paid back from the savings on energy bills. Chris Huhne, Energy and Climate Change Secretary says, 'It is about making people feel as warm as toast in their homes. I want Britain to say goodbye forever to leaky lofts and chilly draughts.' The scheme requires participating householders to take part in a three-step plan.

- **Step One** – to have an independent energy survey of the property, providing clear advice on the best energy-efficient options to the building.
- **Step Two** – Green Deal finance to be provided by a range of accredited providers, which will be repaid through savings on energy bills, making properties cheaper to run from day one.
- **Step Three** – homes will then receive their energy efficient package. Only accredited measures will be installed by appropriately qualified installers giving consumers confidence that the deal they are getting is high quality and will save money.

Green Deal promises to put money-saving energy efficiency measures within the financial reach of many individuals for the first time. It offers the potential to open up a whole new market for energy-efficient materials and equipment.

Elsewhere in the world, there are varying levels of financial support for Green Roof projects. It may take the form of tax reductions, reduced water bills or occasionally a contribution to installation costs. Any support programme does require that the green roof has to meet specific criteria such as stormwater run-off, insulation and biodiversity.

3 GREEN ROOFS IN USE – BUSINESS

Green roofs are being adopted by businesses of all kinds. With new build business developments, green roofs are often being requested as a condition of the planning permission. This is because the roof is seen as a way of replacing the green environment lost on the ground. Other advantages that are popular with businesses include reduced energy usage and thus lower costs; decreased noise levels inside buildings; the fact that a green roof can extend the life of a roof; and reduced risk of flooding. The green roof on a business development is seen as an important element of a sustainable energy building.

For example, The Paradise Park Children's Centre in London was built with a green roof and a green wall exterior providing insulation and extra evaporative cooling. Richard Pearce, building services engineer is quoted in the 2008 Living Roofs and Walls Technical Report as saying:

> The depth of the roof is approximately 150mm (6in). The thermal mass slows the transfer of the heat through the roof by up to six hours. The highest gain through a flat roof in the summer is at noon; the maximum flow of heat through the roof is therefore during early evening. As the building normally closes at 5pm, the occupants will no longer be overheated in the building, so obviating the need for air conditioning.

Green roofs are changing the urban landscape making cities greener and more pleasant for everyone. In London's Docklands, the tiered roofs of New Providence Wharf make an eye-catching sight, adding greenery in a built-up area. As Marc Deeley, of Thames Gateway Sustainable Development Team points out:

> Installing living roofs in our existing urban environment will not only help us adapt to a changing climate. It will also create a new urban landscape that can be enjoyed by people through direct access or as an alternative view from the office window. Some living roofs can even be designed to provide us with food, so the potential for city regions to develop and implement these technologies could create thousands of sustainable jobs at the same time.

The experience of cities around the world would indicate that the height of a roof does not matter – green roofs are being installed on skyscrapers just as successfully as on lower roofs. Nor does the pitch of a roof make much of a difference – green roofs are being placed on flat roofs as well as roofs with a pitch of 30 or more degrees.

One of the oldest green roofs in the UK business community is found on the Grade one listed Willis Building in Ipswich. Built in 1974, as a headquarters building for the Willis Faber insurance group; the company aimed to restore a sense of community to the workplace. As a result the decision was made to install a roof garden. The rooftop garden covers the majority of the roof space and comprises a lush green lawn and a neat privet hedge. Director of Communications Ingrid Booth comments:

> The rooftop garden is very popular with our staff who enjoy having their lunch outside in the summer months and taking in the views over the town. We also hold a number of staff and

OPPOSITE: Bagot goats grazing on a green roof over a coffee shop in Northumberland.

Tiered green roofs overlooking London's Docklands. (Photo: Alumasc)

fundraising events up there. We had Olympic swimmer Mark Foster giving our staff, who were taking part in the Great Eastern Swim, some tips in a giant inflatable pool during their lunch break.

In 2010, a green roof was installed on the seventh floor of the city of London headquarters belonging to international law firm Eversheds. While in Hanover, the Norddeutsche Landesbank has installed 5,000m^2 of green roof. This is made up of 3,500m^2 of extensive roof, plus 1,500m^2 of intensive roof. According to project landscape architect Volker Lange, the key element was aesthetic design 'not to simply green the building by using a lot of plants but to design a platform which compliments the building structure'. The plants are placed in specific order to indicate direction, link lines, shapes and materials. Intensive vegetation in the shape of round plant islands integrated into red cedarwood decks were placed beside the company restaurant. Siemens AG set out to improve the view from adjacent buildings by adding a green roof of rockery-type plants onto their staff canteen. Constructed in 1991, the Japanese roof garden at Mitsui-Yamaha Motor company, Neuss, aimed to screen parked cars from the view of offices overlooking the inner courtyard.

One of the more unusual green roofs on business properties has been created at Tirol, where 9,700m^2 of roof space over underground garages at the Aquadome have been used to develop an extensive roof garden. Bushes and shrubs are planted around vents to help camouflage technical equipment. Trees planted at a lower level have been allowed to grow through the ceiling and emerge on the roof. Safety grids are used to cover the surface between tree and roof surface.

Planning requirements, aesthetics and drainage improvements are key reasons why businesses are installing green roofs. Often there is a requirement for businesses to blend into the environment. Developments at the Woolwich Arsenal had to have a landscaped green roof so as not to distract from the historic buildings. In Stranraer, Scotland, the Gallie Craig Coffee Shop was required to have a green roof to meet planning approval. The location of the shop is on a cliff overlooking the Mull of Galway and is in an area of outstanding natural beauty.

HOTELS AND CATERING

Growing vegetables on the roof and using the fresh produce in meals is becoming popular with hotels and catering establishments, particularly in North America. The Fairmont Hotel, Vancouver has a 2,100ft^2 roof garden, in which grow over sixty varieties of herbs, vegetables and fruits. It has even added a honey bee apiary. Guests can book a guided tour of the garden and apiary, as well as request rooms overlooking or with access to the garden.

SCHOOLS AND EDUCATIONAL ESTABLISHMENTS

More and more schools and educational sites are opting for green roofs, changing concrete cubes into living environmental education. The opportunity to use roofs for teaching and research purposes has been a key motivator for many schools adopting a green roof policy. Sharrow School in Sheffield is one of the most well-known examples with its extensive roof gardens across several levels. On a smaller scale, there are schools like North Harringay Primary School in London, which turned the roof of the gymnasium into a

The Gallie Craig roof blends smoothly into its coastal location. (Photo: Alumasc)

The green roof at Woolwich Arsenal. (Photo: Alumasc)

roof garden which is used for teaching and community purposes. In Ohio, USA a children's nursery has built a sedum-covered porch occupying 75ft stretching over the entrance and adjoining barn. The roof is edged with plastic pots filled with cascading petunias and other annuals, while the remainder of the roof is a sod roof. The containers are held in place by extruded aluminium edging with slots in it so that water can drain away. On the north side of the barn, a waterfall slopes down from the roof through a collection of boulders. Over in Northern France, the Lycée Jean Moulin has been built with a series of undulating green roofs terraced into the hillside.

In the US, many schools are seeking to link science studies with green roofs. Albemarle High School, Charlottesville is a good example of this. It has over 33,000ft^2 of green roofs across its buildings and incorporates a real- time monitoring system that checks the roof's water content, temperature and moisture levels. Lindsay Snoddy, environmental compliance manager for Albemarle County Public Schools states 'science classes are able to utilize data from the green roof monitoring system to investigate the benefits of the green roof related to thermal insulation. With additional instrumentation, the stormwater benefits could also be explored by students.'

The Boston Latin School has taken the educational concept to its widest extent. On top of its roof there is a weather station, greenhouse, two outdoor classrooms, a cafeteria, a garden, solar panels and a wind turbine. The whole 70,000ft^2, $6.2 million green roof complex is the idea of students at Boston Latin School. 'It started out as a simple request for how the school can reduce its carbon footprint,' said architect Gail Sullivan, 'but then the students said yes, yes, and yes to all the different features.' Unfazed by the price, students from the school's Youth Climate Action Network spent a year raising money and applying for grants to create their green roof. The garden now includes 350 trays of sedum, plus a twenty-eight solar panel array. It has become an integral part of the school curriculum, for example, students measure wind speed and test how much power the solar panels are generating, and learn how to grow food in the rooftop greenhouse for use in the cafeteria. English and art classes find inspiration from the rooftop orchard and garden. The roof complex is also influencing other schools in the area. Students from the Youth Climate Action Network have worked with Boston area teachers to develop a middle school and high school sustainability curriculum based around their rooftop experiences. The roof has become a 'learning laboratory' designed to integrate sustainability education.

At higher education level, universities and colleges have taken up the concept mainly as a means of conducting research, reducing energy costs and improving the environment. This has become a major drive in their use of green roof technology. Because of the multidimensional nature of green roofs, it offers research possibilities from horticulture to landscape and building architecture, engineering, urban planning and policy. Researchers are experimenting in laboratories, field testing on roofs and creating computer modelling systems. For example, Pennsylvania State University has covered over an acre of its buildings with green roofs and is currently in the process of doubling that amount both through new constructions and retrofits. As Dr Robert Berghage, from the Department of Horticulture points out:

> Not only do we research here, but we have a lot of roofs so we're big users as well. A lot of what is driving this is LEED, but that's not the only driver. We're also interested in the longevity of our roofs and stormwater issues on certain parts of campus.

Students at the University of London began work on analysing green roof effects when a new roof was added above a block of council flats in Camden. In 2010, a green roof was installed on the new performing arts centre at Leeds University. Constructed by Sedum Supply, the 110m^2 roof covers three different areas with a

University of Suffolk, Ipswich, waterfront building. (Photo: Bauder)

varying roof pitch of between 2 degrees to 5 degrees. The roof is not designed for public access, just to be seen from overlooking buildings.

In Ipswich, the University Campus Suffolk has a green roof with a 20 degree pitch. The distinctive sloping roof on a six-storey building was designed to reflect the location on the waterfront. The roof had to be tapered to two storeys at the rear, street-facing facade to link in with existing listed buildings. Design considerations were a key motivator in the creation of the green roof, along with energy efficiency. In the Lebanon, a green roof on the American University of Beirut is designed to provide a quiet retreat for students as well as being a way in which the benefits of green roofs can be demonstrated.

Sustainability was the main driver for the Jubilee Three teaching centre at Easton College, Norwich. The building has become one of the most energy-efficient education buildings in the region. It forms part of a complex set around a garden court with twenty-eight teaching rooms, a sixty-four seat lecture theatre, café, laboratories and offices. The framework of the building comprises glulam beams and concrete so as to retain maximum heat overnight ensuring classrooms are warm when classes start in the morning. The south-facing wall is completely glazed and provides natural daylight all year round. Overhanging eaves, woven with ornamental vines, help to cool and shade the building in summer, and increase the warmth of the building in winter. The sloping green roof is planted with 17,500 sedum plants, wild thyme and wild strawberries designed to encourage biodiversity, add insulation and decrease stormwater run-off.

RETAIL OUTLETS

Retail outlets have shown a mixed reaction to green roofs. The Kensington Roof Gardens are one of the most well-known green roofs established over a retail outlet. In Norwich, Norfolk, the Castle Mall Shopping Centre was constructed in a sensitive location near a historic castle. Most of the centre is below ground, and covered with a public park complete with paths, shrubs, lawns, trees and a children's play area.

A grocery store with a green roof. (Photo: East of England Co-Op)

Elsewhere in the UK, the use of green roofs on individual retail buildings has been limited. There are grocery stores, such as the East of England Co-Op food store at Hatfield Peverel which has a $350ft^2$ green roof. The company states that it decided to choose a sedum roof for planning considerations since it would provide greenery where there was none in the area. In addition, the roof would moderate water run-off from the roof, reduce solar heat gain and create a visually pleasing surface at first floor level. Most of the roof can be accessed directly from the first floor and watering is undertaken by hand whenever it becomes necessary. The roof has a 15 degree pitch and is covered with a 19mm (8½in) ply deck on trussed rafters while the flat areas of the roof have a concrete base. The sedum blanket on a growing substrate is placed over high density, rigid foam insulation and Decothane Root Resistant waterproofing. Garden centres such as Dobbies have begun introducing green roofs over the entrance to some of their centres.

By far the greatest retail use has been in Europe where green roofs have been used to considerable effect. Enschede in the Netherlands has a $1,000m^2$ green roof on top of a department store. Part of the roof has been built on to create two floors of apartments and there is a green roof in the middle which is used by residents. Not far away the new build De Klanderij shopping mall in Enschede has had a complete residential street with gardens created 6m above the ground. Residents can drive their cars direct to their home on top of the mall, park in front, walk through their

OPPOSITE: A green roof prevented the shopping centre from intruding on a sensitive location in Norwich.

Dobbies Garden Centre, Aberdeen. (Photo: Dobbies)

own garden to reach their front doors. In total there is 9,000m^2 of paving, lawn and trees.

In Arhus, Denmark, the Brunns Galleri shopping mall has a 1,600m^2 green roof. Building the green roof did pose a problem as wind uplift was a major issue. The 10m high building is close to the harbour. In order to prevent the sedum plants being blown off, a vegetation-free granite area was installed to provide ballast at the edges of the roof.

One of the most extensive green roofs on a retail development has been created at the Mag Galleries, in Geislingen, Germany. The 10,000m^2 shopping development has a green roof that was chosen to blend in with the historic town as well as providing a range of public amenities. The roof is accessed via lifts, stairs, footbridges and ramps and includes a lawn, hardy plants, shrubs, trees, benches, play facilities and a 650m^2 basketball court.

DISTRIBUTION

The acres of roof space presented by distribution are regarded as ideal for green roofs. These are buildings that frequently have few aesthetic qualities, and green roofs are seen as a way of making them blend into the landscape.

One of the largest green roofs created in Britain is over the Adnams Brewery Distribution Centre in Southwold, Suffolk. The centre comprises a large single-storey 4,400ft^2 warehouse located in a disused gravel pit set within 85 acres of grassland. The roof covers 0.6 hectares. Having a roof that would blend into the landscape was regarded as important. The building is very environmentally friendly. The walls are made of lime and hemp blocks, while the roof is a huge curve supported on glulam (glued and laminated) timber beams running approximately 60m across the building. These are the longest ever glulam beams to be used in the UK and it provides a 35m column of free space within the main warehouse. Sedums were chosen for the roof vegetation, as this would best enhance the setting and promote biodiversity. The sedum roof is linked to a sustainable urban drainage system designed to collect rainwater as Adnams aim to harvest most of the water used on site. Keeping the interior of the building free of extreme temperature fluctuations is essential to ensure the beer is stored in a good condition. The green roof is seen as an

Adnams Distribution Centre, Southwold. (Photo: Adnams)

integral part of the overall environmental and energy-saving policy for the building. Research has shown that the combination of green roof, insulation properties of the lime/hemp walls, glulam beams and passive ventilation are keeping temperatures at the right level without additional help. Adnams say that the building was about 15 per cent more expensive than a traditional metal box warehouse, but the company believe that this additional investment will be justified in the long term by significantly lower energy usage and greater operational efficiency.

PUBLIC ORGANIZATIONS

Government, municipal and other public organizations are using green roofs to provide new areas of greenery. Sometimes the public may not even

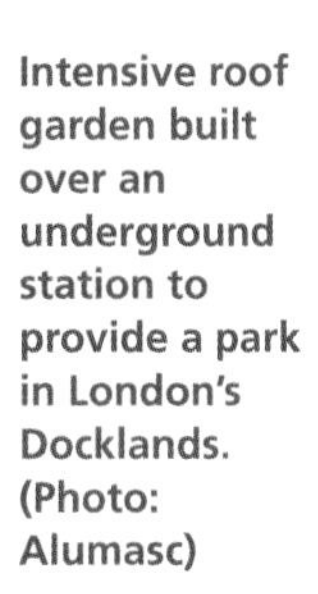

Intensive roof garden built over an underground station to provide a park in London's Docklands. (Photo: Alumasc)

be aware that it is a green roof rather than just a public green space. Most people in Norwich forget that part of the Castle Gardens covers a shopping mall while the rest is a former moat. In Linz, Austria for example, the Bindermichl Motorway Tunnel has been covered with an 8.13 hectare park while in London, the Tower of London installed a green roof over the Tower Gift Shop, creating a park-like setting where the public could sit and enjoy the historic site. Canary Wharf, London has Jubilee Park, a 22,000m^2 public park built over an underground station complete with fountains, paths, water- bound walkway, shrubs, trees and lawn. Underground car parks are frequently being given green roofs to provide parkland. Typical examples are the Park de Rietlanden, Amsterdam where a 5,700m^2 public park with playgrounds, lawns and trees have been created on top of an underground car park; and Sittard in the Netherlands where the renovation of the City Hall offered an opportunity to create an underground car park with a roof that has become a public park with lawns, rhododendrons and large trees.

Looking at buildings that have been covered with more traditional green roofs, it is clear that they are widespread on a worldwide basis covering both large and small public buildings. In the United States, the Public Health department in Salt Lake City Utah has a 2,500ft^2 section of the roof covered with eight varieties of sedum plants. Over in Milwaukee, the Columbia St Mary's Hospital received a $325,000 grant from the Milwaukee Metropolitan Sewerage District Regional Green Roof Initiative Programme to construct a 6,000ft^2 green roof above the hospital atrium and a 12,400ft^2 green roof on a separate building. While in San Francisco, the Steinhart Aquarium and Morrison Planetarium have a 2.5 acre green roof filled with native plants. Part of the domed roof has a 45 degree pitch and required the use of rock-filled baskets to deal with drainage. Nearly half a million native California plants were used in the planting including beach strawberry (*Fragaria chiloensis*), sea thrift (*Armeria maritima*), self-heal (*Prunella vulgaris*), Pacific stonecrop (*Sedum spathfolium*), California poppy (*Eschscholzia californica*), miniature lupin (*Lupinus bicolour*), goldfields (*Lasthenia californica*) and California plantain. In Budapest, Hungary, the Living Danube waste water treatment project has been given a 10,000m^2 green roof. In London, the Museum of London has greened all its roofs. Thousands of square yards of green roofs will be used on the buildings used for the London 2012 Olympics.

Charities too are looking at the concept with interest. The UK's largest dog welfare charity, Dogs' Trust, is building a sustainable energy Rehoming Centre in Leicestershire. Built on 14 acres of farmland previously used for intensive pig farming, the centre will incorporate green roofs, underfloor heating, solar thermal panels, photovoltaic panels and a rainwater recycling system. Green roofs are seen as integral part of the energy mix so as to achieve the highest possible levels of sustainability. Dogs' Trust Property Director, Matthew Taylor says 'Our desire is to design our buildings with the emphasis on reducing, as far as possible, the energy demands that these new Rehoming Centres require, through mass insulation, improved air tightness and natural ventilation systems'.

LEISURE USE

Wildlife and environmental charities frequently use green roofs within nature reserves. Bird hides and sheds are often covered with sedum or turf.

Green roofs are ideal for leisure areas, particularly public parks and golf courses where roofs and buildings have to blend into the environment. On a much smaller scale, architects ID Partnership designed green roofs for twenty beach huts in Blyth, Northumberland. The pitched roofs each measure 2.5×3.5m and have a 40mm (1½in) growing medium. A special galvanized metal edge trim has had to be installed on each roof in order to keep the 250m^2 of sedum and substrata in place.

Even cruise ships have introduced green roofs. Several Royal Caribbean Cruise ships have green roofs providing a place for guests to relax and play lawn games even when they are in the middle of

Green roof at the Sainsbury Centre for visual Arts, Norwich.

the ocean. The high quality turf has had to cope with forty-foot waves and wind speeds of over 100 miles per hour.

MIXED USE DEVELOPMENTS

A good example of the way in which green roofs are being used as a way of improving the environment and providing biodiverse habitats can be seen at Deptford Creek in South East London. In this area, a combination of brown and green roofs are being added to buildings of varying sizes and functions.

Deptford Creek comprises a major Thames-side area that for many years had been mainly occupied by derelict factories and wharfs. A major brown field development site, it had provided the perfect environmental conditions for rare species such as the black redstart. When plans for the redevelopment of the area were drawn up, environmentalists successfully insisted that any redevelopment must include substantial environmental provision including green roofs.

As a result, the area is set to become the largest cluster of green roofs in the UK with around 3,600ft^2 across several neighbouring buildings.

The Laban Dance centre incorporates a 600m^2 green roof. The largest part of the roof is made of varying depths of crushed brick and concrete and was sown with an annual wildflower mix to give an immediate impact. After the initial sowing, it has been left to develop naturally. The second part of the roof is covered with volcanic pellets

An example of local authority use in a country park.

that will attract mosses and lichens. This part of the roof can be viewed through glass panels.

Green Reach 2000 is a retail and housing complex. The roof will include 200m^2 of brick and concrete for natural colonization by wildflowers and mosses plus an area measuring 300m^2 covered by sedum matting.

Four other major schemes in the area include green roofs totalling about 2,500m^2. In each scheme about 65 per cent of the roof will be green. One scheme seeking planning permission includes over 1,000m^2 of green roof space (95 per cent of the total roof area) that includes a collection of boulders and pieces of old timber. It is believed that this will add to the visual effect and also provide a varied setting in which to encourage biodiversity. All the roofs throughout the Deptford Creek cluster will include nesting structures for birds such as black redstart, sand martin and kingfisher.

There are many mixed-use developments elsewhere in the world. A good example is in Finsenvej, Copenhagen. This development comprises a supermarket on the ground floor, followed by two floors of car parking, then the offices of an architecture firm with its own roof garden and terrace. The top floor is occupied by penthouses surrounded by a security belt of sedum vegetation outside the fences.

TRANSPORT

Transport is proving to be a big user of green roofs in all shapes and forms. It may be a simple matter of greening the environment or as part of a wider sustainability programme to build the most

View of terrace and roof garden at Finsensvej. (Photo: Ulrik Reeh Veg Tech)

Close-up of the Finsensvej terrace showing the green roof on the storage unit. (Photo: Ulrik Reeh Veg Tech)

Green roofs at London's Rotherhithe Tube Station. (Photo: John Sturrock)

energy-efficient buildings possible. Network Rail have announced plans for a new headquarters building in Milton Keynes which will use a range of measures designed to regulate temperature and reduce energy usage including high overhanging soffits to provide shade and natural ventilation, and extensive living roofs to encourage biodiversity. Rainwater harvesting systems will be used to flush toilets and irrigate the plants.

To take another example, the refurbished Rotherhithe station on the London Overground East London Route has had part of its building covered with a sedum roof. Transport for London (TfL) Director of London Overground Infrastructure, Peter Richards says, 'Building this crucial new rail link between north and south London brought many challenges and we were determined to come up with as many environmentally friendly solutions to them as possible.' The roof is on five levels covering 140m^2 and is visible through wide panoramic windows to passengers as they travel down to the platforms on the escalators. 'This particular model is unusual among living roofs in that it will be highly visible to passengers and part of their journey scenery as opposed to being perched up high and out of sight,' commented architect Richard Aylesbury.

Elsewhere in London, the UK's largest, greenest bus garage was opened in West Ham. The garage houses 320 buses and has a range of eco-friendly features including a green sedum roof and a wind turbine. The building has been designed to be as sustainable as possible and to avoid the wasteful use of natural resources. The garage is predicted to cut CO_2 emissions by 27 per cent compared to a building built with traditional materials. The sedum roof is regarded as an integral part of the sustainability building programme alongside other green features such as a laminated timber roof structure, rainwater harvesting, natural ventilation minimizing the

Construction of the green roof on West Ham Bus Garage, London. (Photo: Blackdown Horticultural Consultants)

Barrel-shaped green roofs forming a cover for the West Ham Bus Garage, London. (Photo: John Sturrock)

need for air conditioning, biomass boilers, skylights and bus washing facilities which recycle 70 per cent of the water being used.

HOSPITALS

The creation of tranquil havens and pleasant views to help patient care are just two of the reasons why hospitals are looking at the potential offered by green roofs. In the US, more hospitals are adding roof gardens as a way of improving patient care. The aim is to create tranquil oases such as that at the Betty H. Cameron Women's and Children's Hospital, Wilmington; it has a green roof offering a refuge, fresh air and sunshine to children and families. The Schwab Rehabilitation Hospital, Chicago added a green roof to allow patients to practise real life skills within the confines of the garden. The provision of outdoor space helps relieve tension and gives patients access to the restorative properties of nature, and staff can use the roof as a way of conducting special therapy programmes so that patients do not feel trapped inside the hospital. In New Jersey, the Hackensack University Medical Centre has installed a 4,000ft^2 green roof and demonstration vegetable garden on top of its cancer centre enabling patients to relax in a green space and learn about gardening while waiting for treatment.

MULTI-USE ROOFS

Businesses are looking at ways in which green roofs can be put to more than one use. In Athens, a clothing company has built a green roof which can be used as an open-air catwalk. The roof is designed in stripes with corridors connecting the open spaces. As the garden needed to look good all year round, each stripe was planted with just one variety of grass – *Pennisetum orientale* 'Morning light', *Penisetum setaceum rubrum*, *Miscanthus sinensis* 'Morning light', *Nassela tennuisima.* There are also several trees to add height and shade – *Cercis siliquastrum*, *Prunus omygdalus*, *Prunus cerasifera* and *Pissardi nigra.* Another good example of this multi-use is in Singapore where the first drive-through roof garden has been created, enabling the public to view cars from the Subaru showroom in a rooftop setting.

In Dusseldorf, Germany the BMW building has installed an intensive green roof complete with shrubs, bushes, trees and a miniature lake set around a penthouse suite. Conference rooms and offices open onto the green roof, and it is used as a site for open-air business meetings. Likewise, the Lauer offices at Unterensingen, Germany have intensive landscaping on three lower roof levels and extensive landscaping on the upper roof. The intensive roofs are used by employees for conference meetings and relaxation areas during breaks.

TALL BUILDINGS

The height of many urban office buildings does pose a challenge for the installation of green roofs. The heat island effect is strongest in cities and this is where most tall office buildings are to be found. Wind speed adds to the difficulties since these double for every ten stories of a building's height. Windy conditions increase moisture loss in plants, so drought-tolerant plants do tend to survive best on tall buildings. On buildings of twenty storeys and more, roofs are subject to constant wind. One of the biggest problems faced by plants in those circumstances is dehydration and wind chill – if the soil is frozen too long, plants cannot extract moisture from the soil and are unable to replace moisture lost due to wind chill.

Technology and ingenuity is providing some answers to the problems such as when installing a green roof on a 50m-high building at Zurich Airport Kloten Parking Garage B. Specially designed lorries were used to pump substrate onto the roof using a pneumatic pump. A jute net had to be added to protect plants against the strong winds. In the USA, the Sears Tower is being refurbished to make it much more energy efficient. Green roofs are regarded as a key element in this $300 million project to green the tallest building in the western hemisphere. Now renamed the Willis Tower, the size of the building means that a change in the direction of the sun can result in air conditioning being pumped into one part of the building while the side in shadow is being heated. As part of the programme, a green roof has been installed on the ninetieth floor. This required metal meshing to prevent the soil and plants from being blown away. The sedum on the roof is flourishing even at that height – and is being visited by ladybirds!

Access is another problem that has to be considered when installing green buildings within cities. Streets cannot be closed off, and installation of materials may have to take place very early in the morning. The problems surrounding construction of the Toronto Podium roof is a good example of this situation. Construction work had to stop whenever the council sessions were in progress, and it was also necessary to work around the programme of public events in the square. Materials were frequently loaded and unloaded at 5am in the morning, and as the Podium could not be sealed off during the day contractors had to be continually watching for members of the public strolling up the outdoor ramp from the square below to see what was happening.

Payback is possibly the greatest difficulty for many businesses. The costs of installing a green roof are higher than a conventional one. A major scheme such as the greening of the Willis Tower in Chicago in which green roofs form part of a wider environmental energy reduction project is expected to take up to twenty-six years to see a payback on the investment.

4 GREEN ROOFS INTERNATIONAL

Green Roofs have become an international phenomenon as energy prices rise and the problems of climate change become more apparent. In addition, increasing population numbers are forcing the attention of planners into investigating ways of maximizing usage of all available space, including roofs. Bare roof space has become too valuable to be left untouched. Roofs can be put to many uses – amenity space, playgrounds, sporting facilities, cafes, farms, gardens.

A World Green Roof Infrastructure Network was formed in 2008. Membership now includes Australia, Brazil, Canada, France, Germany, Mexico, USA, Spain, Italy, New Zealand, Greece, Peru and Russia. The extent to which green roofs have been utilized does vary from country to country – in some countries, like Germany, they are long established while in others, such as Australia, green roofs are fairly new. What is noticeable is the speed at which they are being adopted, and adapted to local needs. There is an explosion of interest worldwide – a 2010 Building Expo in China saw more than 80 per cent of the 240 structures on show use large-scale greenery in roof-top gardens and green-walled exteriors. Typical of the offerings were:

- Singapore – a roof garden with more than 100 tropical plants, fountains, palms and ferns.
- New Zealand – a mini-park on a sloping roof with plants ranging from plateau vegetation to tree ferns and desert plants as well as vegetables showing just what can be grown within the country.
- Shanghai – plants cover the roof and walls, using movable green panels.
- Switzerland – a 4,000m^2 rooftop lawn
- India – grasses and flowers of different colours adorn the roof of the pavilion
- Hong Kong – rooftop woods comprising forty trees such as banyan and osmanthus.

OPPOSITE: **Rooftop flowers at the Vancouver Convention Center. (Photo: PWL Partnership)**

This chapter aims to give an outline of what is happening in a selection of countries highlighting any legislative requirements and interesting projects. It does not set out to be an exhaustive study of green roofs in every country worldwide. Only a few countries such as Germany have specific building guidelines that apply to green roofs. Elsewhere, construction of green roofs is covered under general building and roofing regulations. High buildings may be subject to extra regulations about security and wind resistance.

ARGENTINA

Buenos Aires is a highly built-up city, possessing just 2m^2 of green space per inhabitant. This falls far short of the 10m^2 recommended by the World Health Organization. Green roofs are seen as a way of increasing this available green space. In addition, the urban heat island effect causes significant problems and, as a result, the local authorities are making tax breaks available to encourage the construction of green roofs. Sedum roof gardens are being constructed on municipal buildings and it is intended to link these with water channel and solar collector systems to improve energy savings.

AUSTRIA

One of the biggest success stories in terms of green roof installation is the city of Linz. The economic boom of the 1960s and 1970s resulted in what has been recognized as an environmental disaster due to the massive growth in the steel and chemical industries. This resulted in a huge loss of agricultural land and deterioration in the quality of life. In the 1980s the town planners set out to reclaim green space within the city by introducing green roof projects. Preference was always given to the planting of trees, bushes, low plants and grass on roofs. Since 1985, all building plans have an integral green roof element. Green roofs have been installed on warehouses, public buildings, council housing, private housing and apartment blocks. By far the largest green roof project is the Bindermichl Motorway Tunnel, which forms an 8.13 hectare public park. This project has provided an answer to the problems of divided communities, noise and air pollution. By building a tunnel over the motorway, it enabled the town authorities to create a public park full of grass, trees, flowers, walkways and seating areas. The park provides a link between the two sides of a housing estate that had previously been divided by the motorway.

AUSTRALIA

The most well-known example of a green roof in Australia was established as long ago as 1988. Parliament House in Canberra has a green roof designed to preserve the shape of the hill into which the building was developed. Over the past ten years, roof gardens on existing commercial buildings have begun to appear. A ten-storey office block in Melbourne has turned a blank expanse of concrete on its roof into a pleasant recreational space. Hardy succulents, native flowering plants and grasses grow alongside a herb garden, lemon and olive trees, and wisteria and passion fruit vines. There is also a built-in barbecue, gazebo and a picket fence around the perimeter. The food the garden produces is used by the small businesses that occupy the building which include an art gallery, language centre and Open Universities Australia. The paving is made of permeable recycled glass that filters rainwater into the building's green roof system. The whole project cost around $250,000. The Victorian Desalination Project has a living tapestry of 98,000 native plants in its 26,000m^2 green roof.

There have been major green roof studies investigating the suitability of native plants to green roof developments, undertaken by various Universities. The University of Melbourne conducted several years of trials linking in with the development of a green roof on the Venny building. In Victoria, the State Government has helped fund a study into adapting green roof technology to local conditions. Central Queensland University is undertaking an innovative study linking with Brisbane and Rockhampton to investigate how rooftop gardens can process restaurant food waste through the use of worm farms. The nutrients gained as a result of the worm farms are being used to grow fresh produce on roofs.

CANADA

The green roof movement in Canada is very much led by the City of Toronto. The city is an urban heat island, with extreme summer temperatures. Green roofs are seen as a way of dealing with this problem. In May 2009, Toronto City Council passed a green roof by-law. This law affects all new residential, institutional and commercial building permit applications made after January 31 2010, and January 2011 for all new industrial development. The requirements are compulsory on all new developments above 2,000m^2 of floor space. Under the terms of the by law, up to 50 per cent of all roof space on multi-unit residential dwellings over six storeys, schools, non- profit housing, commercial and industrial buildings has to be green.

Building owners can opt to seek a variance on the by law – but this costs them $200 per m^2 in lieu of installing a green roof. The funds raised as a result of this legislation are being used to pay for an Eco-Roof incentive programme designed to retrofit green roofs on existing buildings. Under

Panorama of the Vancouver Convention Center. (Photo: VCC PWL Partnership)

the terms of the programme, owners who install a green roof on an existing building can apply for a subsidy of $50 per m^2 up to a maximum of $50,000.

The success of this policy, encouraging the widespread introduction of green roofs throughout Toronto, could have a long-term effect. It has been estimated that it could save the city between $40 million and $120 million in stormwater infrastructure costs and reduce the urban heat island effect by lowering temperatures by up to 2°C.

The number and variety of roof projects is extensive. It ranges from major projects such as the 37,000ft^2 roof covering the Podium outside Toronto City Hall to the Hugh Garner Co-Op where the 350 member residents voted to build a green roof in 2004. The Co-Op won an Ontario Trillium Foundation Grant of $100,000 to begin the project, before gaining $150,000 from the Live Green Toronto Grant Programme to proceed with Phase 2 of the development. Additional funding came from corporations, private citizens and the community. The resultant green roof incorporates electro-mechanical technology for preserving rainwater. The design features pergolas and a gazebo for shade. There are also planted beds, accessible raised planters, barrier-free paths, decking and seating. No structural strengthening was needed to the building to allow public access. ESRI Canada adopted a different approach when building a green roof for its Toronto offices. It set up a roof garden on a ninth floor terrace to give an additional 7,500ft^2 of usable space for staff and visitors. The roof is now used for corporate gatherings and staff lunch breaks. Drainage facilities ensure that up to 75 per cent of summer rain is captured for further use.

Elsewhere in Canada, the Vancouver Winter Olympics in 2010 provided a spur to green roof construction. The Olympic Village in Vancouver's False Creek area included green roofs with self-sustaining rainwater collection systems on all its buildings while the media centre based in what has become Vancouver Convention Center had a dramatic green roof installed.

CZECH REPUBLIC

One of the most interesting green roof projects in the Czech Republic is at the Business Technology Park, Prague where a 7,500m^2 scheme was installed in 1999. The intensive roof style was built above an underground garage with substrate depths varying from 200mm to 1,000mm (8in to 40in). Planting includes lawns, bushes and shrubs with building facades linked into the roof garden by the use of climbing plants. Water features and seating areas encourage regular usage.

CHINA

Green roofs have begun to appear in China. Reasons are varied, but drainage is a key motivator. The most dramatic project is in Suqian City, Jiangsu province where there are plans for a mixed-use development involving green roofed buildings being constructed around the Grand Canal running through the centre of the city. The canal links Hangzhou to Beijing, and is one of the oldest canals in the world, as well as one of the longest at 1,776km. The intention is to create an artificial channel coming off the main canal and this is the main axis around which the development is created. This channel would lead directly into the main atrium of the hotel. Taller buildings would represent mountains, and the intersection between buildings and the water serve as landscapes. The aim is to have green roofs covering

A green roof on a building in Peblinge Dossering, Copenhagen. (Photo: Ulrik Reeh Veg Tech)

Flowers and sloping roofs in Denmark. (Photo: Jens Lindhe)

most of the buildings, capturing rainwater and reducing stormwater run-off into the canal.

Manufacturers Samafil Waterproofing Systems in Shanghai created a 700m^2 intensive roof garden on its office building as a way of demonstrating its waterproofing products. The green roof complete with lawns, shrubs and bushes shows the strength of the waterproofing and highlights just what can be done with the product. The roof garden has become a marketing tool. Also in Shanghai, the Giant Campus project incorporates a landscaped green roof designed to provide thermal mass and reduce cooling expenditure.

DENMARK

In 2010, Copenhagen introduced a new municipal policy requiring all new building plans to incorporate green roofs. The legislation applies to all buildings with roofs that have less than a 30 degree pitched roof. It also applies to older roofs which are undergoing refurbishment and have some form of public financial input. Such older roofs have to be retrofitted with a green roof.

Bo Asmus Kjeldgaard, Copenhagen's Mayor of technical and environmental administration states that:

> Copenhagen has set itself the ambitious target of becoming the world's first carbon neutral capital by 2025. To meet this ambitious goal we need ambitious measures. Therefore we have now decided to ensure the City adapts to extreme weather conditions by making new requirements for getting grass on top as many buildings as possible.

Under the terms of the legislation, green roofs must meet two out of five requirements:

- The roof must absorb 50 to 80 per cent of rainwater run-off
- Provide winter insulation and summer cooling effect and reduce reflection as this has a positive effect on the quality of life and design of the city
- Reduce the heat island effect within Copenhagen
- The roof must double the life of the roofing membrane.

Developers can choose which type of green roof they wish to use. The only let out clause will be if the building is architecturally spectacular and meeting other city requirements.

As a result of this decision, the number of green roofs in Copenhagen is set to increase. By 2010, the city had 20,000m^2 of green roofs and it aims to increase this by 5,000m^2 annually; other towns are investigating the subject. One of the most stunning green-roofed buildings in Copenhagen is the 8 House. This represents one of the largest and most innovative uses of green roofs in Scandinavia. Covering 1,700m^2 of space, each 70m roof covers a long slope descending eleven floors to the edge of a canal in Oerestad South. The roof pitch is quite steep – ranging from 30 to 32 degrees – and is planted up with moss, sedum and native plants. Only the wooden terrace where the step roofs meet, and the stairs along the roof, are accessible to the public. The design aims to open up the interior courtyard to a view of the protected open spaces of Kalvebod Faelled, Denmark. Green spaces upon the roof are strategically placed to reduce the urban heat island effect as well as providing a visual relief to the inhabitants. Industrial buildings increasingly incorporate green roofs such as that on the power plant station near Copenhagen Airport which has a pitch rising from 0 to 35 degrees.

EGYPT

Green roofs with a difference can be found in this country. Soilless roof gardens are common, with plants growing on tables rather than directly onto the roof itself. Vegetables and fruit are widely grown on roofs.

A sedum roof covering the district power plant adjacent to Copenhagen Airport. (Photo: Ulrik Reeh, Veg Tech)

FRANCE

Architects in France are paying increasing attention to the potential offered by green roofs. One of the most unusual uses of a green roof can be seen in Amiens where the Centre de Formation de Football has a training pitch which moves from ground level and curves up and onto the roof which is covered entirely in grass. Identifying where the roof begins and ends in its link with the main pitch is not easy. The large overhangs keep the interior of the building cool in summer, and warm in winter. Over in Les Lucs-Sur-Boulogne, an 8,000m^2 green roof was incorporated into the Museum L'Historial de la Vendee. The roof is carefully designed to blend into the landscape; in spring it resembles a floating prairie.

GERMANY

Extensive green roofs have been planted in Germany since the 1970s. Building codes relating to green roofs have existed since the 1980s. Initially, the aim was to use green roofs to replace open space lost at ground level when new buildings were constructed. This aim has now been partly superseded by a need to use green roofs as part of Sustainable Urban Drainage Schemes dealing with stormwater surges and to reduce flooding. Consumers and businesses are encouraged to install green roofs via legal requirements and a system of grants administered by many local authorities. These grants can pay up to 50 per cent of the additional cost of installing a green roof. Around 43 per cent of German cities offer financial incentives – Berlin, Boblingen, Frankfurt, Karlsruhe, Kassel and Stuttgart have provided grants ranging from E5 to E50 per square metre of green roof. In addition, 17 per cent of German cities also offer reduced sewage disposal charges for developments with green roofs.

Many cities have a legal requirement insisting

A thirty-year-old green roof on Funeral House, Esslingen, Germany. (Photo: ZinCo)

The Hundertwasser Project in Darmstadt. (Photo: Jorg Breuning/Green Roof Service LLG)

on the provision of green roofs on any new, flat-roofed buildings. Munich has introduced legislation regarding the use of roof landscaping in its local development plans. The Federal Nature Conservation Act requires developers to include some mitigation for the ecological impact caused by building – green roofs are the usual criteria. About 14 million m² of green roofs are installed each year. It is estimated that about three quarters of these roofs are extensive, the remaining quarter being intensive roof gardens.

GREECE

Green roofs are fairly new to Greece. One of the most recent was installed on the Greek Ministry of Finance Treasury building in Athens. Described as an 'oikostegi', the roof has been very successful in reducing energy demand and improving air quality. The 650m^2 green roof has created energy savings of E5,630 per annum.

HONG KONG

The Hong Kong government has adopted a positive policy of encouraging green roofs especially on municipal buildings. In 2010, the Secretary for Development Mrs Carrie Lam stated that there were 159 Government buildings with green roofs and a further 114 either planned or in the process of creation. Since 2001, the Architectural Services department has automatically incorporated roof greening into the design of new buildings wherever it was practicable.

In 2006, Jim Chi Yung, a professor at the University of Hong Kong set up a green roof trial on top of one of the skyscraper buildings belonging to the university. The project divided the roof into four sections, one covered with bare concrete, one covered with grass, one covered with a low-growing perennial, and the final section covered with shrubs. Using infrared sensors, Jim Chi Yung determined that all the planted areas were lowering the roof temperature by as much as 26°C. The study has now been expanded to cover an additional roof, in a bid to work out what plants can best survive the intense sunlight and weather conditions experienced on the roofs of Hong Kong.

Green roofs are seen as an ecological necessity providing an answer to urban heat islands, as well as helping the environment. The 150m^2 lawn roof at the Kadoorie Farm and Botanic Garden on top of the admission and gift shop is designed to emphasize ecological and bio-diverse benefits. Both intensive and extensive roofs are being used in Hong Kong. The Integer-Exhibition Pavilion contains a roof garden with lawns, pathways, bushes and shrubs which is used by the public.

ITALY

Green roofs have a long history in Italy, having first appeared with the Romans. New style green roofs have been quite innovative, such as the 20,000ft^2 roof on Environmental Park Turin, which was created on the site of the Fiat building. An intensive roof, it alternates between patches of lawn, shrubs and bushes. Most of the roof is flat, but there is an extra 5,000ft^2 of specially created pitched roof made of expanded polystyrene. The roof is designed to provide ecological compensation for the creation of office buildings.

JAPAN

Green roofs are popular, particularly in Tokyo. It is a means of providing additional green space in overcrowded cities, as well as reducing the heat island effect. Energy costs are another key driver in encouraging the use of green roofs. Design skills are much in evidence, such as in the ACROS Fukuoka building in Fukuoka City. The building was created on the last available green space in the city and on one side incorporates a series of green roofs tumbling down the stepped building, linking into public parkland on the ground. Over 35,000 plants and seventy-six different species are planted in the series of roof gardens. According to the owners, the Takenaka Corporation 'regarding the building as a mountain, and with the beauties of nature as a theme, a space configuration and vegetation configuration was adopted which represents the changes of the four seasons'. While the New Otani Hotel, Tokyo has a roof garden complete with waterfall and pond as well as a rose garden filled with red roses, designed for wedding ceremonies.

The Kyoai Gukuen University has adopted an innovative design for a green roof which keeps open space while providing spectator seating for a nearby playing field. The green roof is slanted towards the playing field to create a viewing area. Vaulted concrete arches support the roof and are hollow at the top, creating strong, water-tight depressions that contain enough soil to support larger species of trees and plants. The dramatic funnel-shaped exhibition centre 'Big Sight' in Tokyo has a green roof which has coped successfully with extreme climatic conditions with strong Pacific winds and salty air.

MEXICO

One of the first green roofs to be used in Mexico is at the Museo del Acero Horno, Monterrey. The area was a brown field site, formerly a steel production facility and the decommissioned blast furnace has been turned into a museum. A green sedum roof helps the museum to blend into the surrounding landscape and reduces the visual impact of the new buildings. The design of the roof is unusual in that the planting pattern is designed to recall the flame emitted from blast furnaces.

A green roof project exists in Mexico City. Known as Azoteas Verdes, the first phase aims to convert 30,000m^2 of downtown roof terraces on government buildings into green roofs. The government intend to introduce green roofs to schools, hospitals and the rooftops of metro stations. Many of these roofs will be open to the public and will be planted up with native species of succulent plants such as Grisium, Rubro, Rinto and some species of Agave. Tax discounts will be available if private owners green at least 30 per cent of a roof.

NETHERLANDS

Water management is the main driver in the Dutch approach to the subject of green roofs – understandably since approximately 60 per cent of the country lies below sea level. Rotterdam is

Sunset view over Singapore taken from the green roof of the Sands Sky Park. (Photo: Marina Bay Sands)

stressing green roofs as part of its Rotterdam Climate Initiative designed to reduce the city's $C0_2$ emissions by 50 per cent and help the city adapt to climate change. It has been estimated that 4,623,000m^2 of roof space in Rotterdam is potentially suitable for green roofs. This includes residential buildings, commercial buildings and municipal buildings. Green roofs are being installed on as many municipal buildings as possible. Subsidies are provided to building owners by the local Council and the Water Board at a rate of 30 Euros per square metre of green roof. Demand is high, resulting in the minimum size of roof that could qualify for a subsidy being reduced from 40m^2 to 10m^2.

The number of green roofs throughout the country is steadily increasing and there are several high profile roofs; for example, in Amsterdam the Museumplein is used for public events. This area includes the grass-covered roof of the Albert Hein supermarket located in the south-west corner of the Museumplein, just across from the Concertgebouw. In November 2010, the area was used for a children's event designed to attract attention to the benefits of green roofs and included activities such as sliding down the roof, and learning how to make a green roof; all of which were undertaken under the eagle eye of Sinterklaas and his Zwarte Piets. Another example is the Educatorium at the University of Utrecht, where a 1,500m^2 roof garden was created planted with sedums and grasses. The

sedums are planted to reflect the floor coverings within building such as a carpet of red flowering sedums divided by a strip of yellow sedums. Schipol International Airport has several green roofs on its various buildings, mostly extensive in style. Within urban areas, residential developments increasingly include roof gardens as a way of providing open spaces, usually with community use.

POLAND

The most important roof garden in Poland is at the University of Warsaw and covers 6,400m^2 of roof above the University Library. Constructed in 1999, the scheme is an intensive one, with lawns, shrubs and bushes. The design is geometrical with lots of square and circular beds. Walkways are made of concrete slabs and act as dividers between the various flower beds. Each flower bed is filled with one single plant variety. Mounds are formed around the skylights creating substrates of between 200mm and 400mm (8in and 16in). Another example of the innovative designs to be found in Poland is the headquarters building of Warta Insurance company. A 1,400m^2 intensive green roof was installed in 2000, over the underground garage. It is a shady area with lots of box hedges and shade-loving plants. Additional greenery is provided by the use of climbing plants growing up the facades of the building. The design aimed to provide a relaxing location for Warta employees and in-corporates trick fountains and special lighting effects.

PHILIPPINES

In September 2009, Quezon City Mayor Feliciano R. Belmonte signed Ordinance 1940 requiring developers of private and publicly owned buildings to reserve 30 per cent of their roof space for plants. The Green Roof Ordinance also includes property tax reductions for homes with green roofs. The introduction of green roofs into the Philippines is still in its infancy, but signs are that numbers will increase fast. SM City North Edsa has introduced a 15,500m^2 Sky Garden, while malls like TriNoma, Market! Market! and Green Belt 5 have added planted roofs.

RUSSIA

A rooftop gardening programme was started in St Petersburg in 1993. It was regarded as an ideal way of producing food in an urban setting. Alexander Gavrilov, Agriculture Director of the Centre for Citizen Initiatives stated:

> in just one district (of St Petersburg) it is possible to grow 2,000 tonnes of vegetables. Our climate is approximately the same as Anchorage, Alaska and we have an average of sixty sunny days a year. Our vegetation period is approximately four months (mid-May to mid-September). We grow leafy greens, potatoes and tomatoes.

It is unknown how many roof gardens actually exist in Russia, but one of the known roof gardens is at Kresty Prison in St Petersburg. The rooftop garden is cultivated by prisoners and helps to provide food for the 10,000 prisoners in the gaol. Rooftop vegetables tested for heavy metal contamination had much lower levels than similar vegetables grown on the ground.

In 1997, a book was produced on the subject of rooftop gardens and more than 800 copies were distributed to administrators, health departments, architects and heads of industry. It was said that the easiest way of getting a rooftop garden going was to persuade an institution to build one.

SINGAPORE

Singapore is seeking to promote itself as a tropical Garden City. Initial guidelines on roof gardens and sky terraces were issued in 1997 as a means of providing public spaces for communal use and enjoyment. The use of sky terraces have been deliberately encouraged as a way in which residents and tenants of a building can socialize, interact and enjoy the communal facilities. Green roofs are well established in Singapore on buildings of all kinds and are frequently used as farms providing fresh vegetables and fruit. The Singapore National Library has several sky gardens as well as vertical green walls. One of the more spectacular designs is the Marina Bay Sands Resort, which has three skyscraper towers connected at the top by a 9,940m^2 green roof. This roof acts as a park complete with jogging paths, gardens, a public observatory and a swimming pool. An equally unusual concept is the Subaru Showroom which opened in 2005. This comprises a 1,300m^2 drive-through roof garden passing static Subaru car displays, a rainforest, grassland, rocky outcrop complete with waterfall, a desert garden and a mountain garden.

A series of initiatives by the Urban Redevelopment Authority and National Parks Board were introduced in 2009 to promote what Singapore describes as 'skyrise greenery'. It is aiming to create an additional 50 hectares of green roofs by 2030. The initiatives are linked to the Government Blueprint for Sustainable Development launched on 27 April 2009. Sky gardens are regarded as an extremely important element due to the intensity of urban development in Singapore. The Landscaping for Urban Spaces and High Rises (Lush) programme requires developers to automatically include greenery and landscape areas equivalent to the space the development has taken up. This space can be at ground level or vertically on terraces and roof gardens. Existing buildings within key development areas will be asked to participate in an incentive scheme to promote rooftop greenery. Cash incentives of up to half the cost of installation of a green roof are made to building owners.

Cheong Koon Hean, chief executive officer of the URA states 'We are committed towards planning for a sustainable quality built environment and ensuring that our city dwellers are never far away from greenery, even with urban growth and high density levity. Despite Singapore being land scarce, greenery can be pervasive in our urban spaces.'

As a result of government policy, almost all new construction in Singapore involves high rise greenery, sky terraces, and green roofs.

SOUTH KOREA

Green roofs have begun to be introduced into this country. The Green Energy Theme Park, which forms the headquarters of the Korea Electric Power Corporation (KEPCO) contains numerous green roofs. The project includes sloping green roofs, integrated with solar power; wind fields; geothermal power and water reclamation schemes. The green roofs help to blend the complex into the surrounding landscape. In Seoul, a 131 acre green roof will cover the Garak Wholesale Market creating a public garden and pathways with space for recreational, sports and cultural activities. Plans have also been announced for a new $185 million city to be built south of Seoul. Green roofs will be extensively used within the new city, which is designed to represent mountains rising from the landscape.

SPAIN

Environmental concerns are the main driving force behind green roof development in Spain. With a hot dry climate, the aim is to restore greenery while reducing temperatures. Typical projects include the Recycling Plant at Vertresa, which has a 6,300m^2 sedum roof. The Banco di Santander headquarters in Madrid, Spain has a 100,000m^2 roof comprising both extensive and intensive styles with the aim of providing a good working environment for staff while mitigating the effects of new build. The roofs are used for business meetings as well as a place to enjoy breaks from work. A similar principle underlies the development of an intensive garden on top of a Madrid underground garage. Paths link small bridges across a network of waterways and vegetation as well as an acacia avenue. The roof helps to cool the area and provide shade.

SWEDEN

Increasing interest is being experienced in Sweden. As in all the Scandinavian countries there is a long history of earth-covered houses. Now the concept is being adapted on a much larger scale. In Malmo, for example, there are two particularly stunning projects. Architects Kjellgren Kaminsky have designed eco-friendly houses for builders Höllviksnäs Förvaltnings AB incorporating a series of green roofs on different levels. While Erik Guidice Architects have designed a new exhibition centre located beside the Malmo Arena. The centre has 19,000m^2 of exhibition halls and the roof is completely covered in vegetation giving the project one of the largest green roofs in Sweden. The Western Harbour area of Malmo used to a heavily polluted industrial area, but this has now changed as it has become known for its sustainable living environment with green roofs much in evidence.

SWITZERLAND

Switzerland is another leading proponent of green roofs, and has one of the oldest existing ones. This was created in 1914 at the Moos Lake water treatment plant, Wollishofen, Zurich. The 30,000m^2 asphalt roof covering the filter tanks was covered with gravel and soil. Seeds already present in the soil germinated and turned the roof into a meadow landscape, housing many rare species such as the Green Winged Orchid (Orchis Morio). Since the 1970s many more green roofs have been constructed such as at the Zurich railway station and the Cantonal hospitals in Basel. In Zurich, all roof areas of airport buildings have to be green in order to reduce the amount of stormwater run-off, and to provide a pleasant view for inbound and outbound flights. The stepped green roof of the Tschuggen Bergoase Hotel, Arosa offers a well-designed roof with a modern slant.

Federal law states that all federal organizations must apply the Swiss Landscape Concept when commissioning or refurbishing federal buildings so that they match natural settings and landscapes. 25 per cent of all new buildings have to be green buildings. Individual towns and states have their own laws – for example, in Basle, a law dating back to 2002 states that all flat roofs have to be green. Building regulations within the city specify details such as the use of native soils and flora, the depth of the growing medium, and the inclusion of mounds to encourage insect life. Furthermore, if the roof is over 1,000m^2, then the developers have to consult the city ecologists on the final design. Aesthetics play a major part in green roof development – the municipality of Wollerau states that riverside apartment buildings should include extensive green roofs.

TAIWAN

In 2007, the Hsi Liu Foundation initiated a green roof project which aimed to install extensive green roofs on buildings. As a result of this initiative, green roofs were installed on Wushing Elementary School Ren Ai Building; Zinyi

The stepped green roof of the Tschuggen Bergoase Hotel, Arosa, Switzerland. (Photo: ZINCO)

Administration Centre, Zinyi Junior High School and Taipei School of Special Education.

TURKEY

Aesthetics dominate a new Mesa hospital development in Ankara, which incorporates a 1,000m^2 green roof on top of an underground garage. The intensive roof includes flowerbeds full of flowers, grasses, shrubs and trees as well as walkways and benches. The garden is accessible to patients and is described as having a healing atmosphere. While at the Kanyon Center, Levent, Istanbul the 'open air mall' has a colourful, landscaped roof with a pedestrian passage that winds its way through like a canyon.

UNITED STATES OF AMERICA

Despite the widespread use of sod houses during the nineteenth century, the green roof movement had little impact in the United States until quite late in the 1990s. This may have been partly due to the folk memories of sod house problems – of nets having to be hung underneath the roofs to catch insects.

The market is still immature by European standards but it is growing extremely rapidly across all types of commercial, municipal and domestic roofs. Innovation too is present with companies looking at ways of growing food on rooftops, establishing massive greenhouses and even bee gardens to increase the population of honeybees. A further impetus to growth is President Obama's American Recovery and Reinvestment Act. American Rivers have carried out a survey entitled Putting Green to Work which analyses how $1.2 billion of green water infrastructure provided by the Act has been spent. Different types of water infrastructure are divided into bright green and green categories. Bright green are the most popular and highly recommended activities – of which green roofs are one of the most important. The report points out that giving green roofs to just 1 per cent of large buildings in America's medium to large cities could create over 190,000 jobs and create billions in revenue to suppliers and manufacturers that produce or distribute green roof materials.

Green roofs are estimated to account for 10 million square feet of space in an overall flat roofing industry that replaces or builds more than 4 billion square foot in North America each year. Many areas such as New York now have a policy of focusing on sustainability when infrastructure repairs or replacements to state buildings are being made. Vegetated green roofs are frequently included when this happens. It is difficult to know just how many rooftop gardens or green roofs of any kind exist, since in most cities there is no permit category specifically for green roofs. A search by the San Francisco Department of Building Inspection identified eighteen projects that would accommodate rooftop gardens, were completed during the period 2001 to 2010, compared with just four during the previous decade. Government organizations frequently include green roofs as a matter of course – Naval Station Norfolk has installed a turf-style green roof; Peterson Air Force Base in the Rocky Mountains of Colorado; as has the Department of Defence office complex in Virginia; and the Tobyhanna Army Depot. The United States Postal Service are seeking to introduce as many green roofs as possible onto its buildings with the aim of reducing the heat island effect. In Manhattan, the USPS has converted the top of the Morgan Mail Processing Facility into a green roof, creating a 2.5 acre site which is the largest green roof in New York City.

In 1999, the Green Roofs for Healthy Cities organization was founded. It links together public and private companies involved in the green roof sector. It became a formal, not for profit, industry association in 2004. Green Roofs for Healthy Cities sets out to increase awareness of the economic, social and environmental benefits of green roofs within North America. Industry standards have been set for design and installation, as well as criteria for minimizing the risk of fire. In 2010, a wind design standard for vegetative roofing systems was developed so as to minimize the risk of wind damage.

In the Green Roofs for Healthy Cities 2010

industry survey, it was revealed that despite the economic downturn, the US green roof industry had continued to show substantial growth. In its Top Ten Cities list, Chicago came top with more than 500,000ft^2 of green roofs, followed by Washington DC with 190,000ft^2. Chicago has been top of the list for more than six years, reflecting its commitment to the sector.

Chicago has set itself the aim of becoming the greenest city in the US, so as to replace its former image as a heavy industrial city. In 2008, Chicago launched a Chicago Climate Action Plan (CCAP). This was a blueprint for lowering greenhouse gas emissions and dealing with the problems of climate change. Five key strategies were identified:

- The provision of energy efficient buildings
- The use of clean and renewable energy sources
- Improved transportation options
- Reduced waste
- Industrial pollution and adaptation.

As a result of this policy, Chicago plans to decrease its carbon footprint substantially, lowering it to 80 per cent below 1990 levels by 2050.

Green roofs are seen as a crucial element in this overall policy. The idea started back in the 1990s when Mayor Richard M. Daley visited Hamburg, Germany and saw the green roofs in that country. Daley sought to replicate this movement in Chicago, with a vision of a new Chicago possessing trees, roofs, green buildings and alleys. Chicago is now America's green roof capital possessing over 600 green roofs totalling over 7 million square feet of roof space. It is very proactive in encouraging developers and home owners to install green roofs. The city authority has even created its own guide to designing rooftop gardens.

A landmark garden exists on the roof of Chicago City Hall. This is a major retrofit example covering 20,300ft^2 of space. The garden is quite spectacular, containing around 20,000 plants of more than 150 varieties including 100 shrubs, forty vines and two trees, one of which is a flowering cherry sitting on a small hill. Most of the plants are low maintenance perennials and are designed to support a honey bee population producing more than 150lb of honey every year.

Only four of the roof gardens in Chicago are open to the general public:

- Chicago Center for Green Technology.
- PepsiCo Rooftop Garden, which includes wind turbines and solar panels in its design so as to be a working example of sustainable architecture and renewable energy use.
- Millennium Park, built over working commuter rail tracks and parking garages. It is filled with grass and trees. The park includes the Lurie Garden designed by Piet Oudolf which has a 15ft high hedge protecting the perennial garden and enclosing it on two sides, and a footbridge over shallow water dividing the garden between light and dark sides.
- Soldier Field, parkland created over the top of an underground parking facility.

Other projects range from small roofs on top of supermarkets to large areas. All types of green roofs are involved, from extensive projects such as the Soldier Field where parkland spreads over an underground parking garage to intensive ones like the Peggy Notabaert Center, which has prairie plants, a small wetland area and a bonsai-style oak tree growing in eight inches of soil on the roof. In San Francisco, a botanic garden is being built on top of the Transbay Transit Garden. Located about 30m off the ground, the garden will include redwood trees and wetlands designed to process grey water, while at the same time capturing all the stormwater which will be stored and used to flush toilets in the buildings. Meanwhile, in Minnesota, the Target Center basketball arena now has a 113,000ft^2 green roof planted with a mix of sedum and prairie plants.

Elsewhere in America, rooftop projects are constantly increasing in number with almost every area and every state showing an interest. Many universities and research organizations are conducting research projects designed to identify which plants are most suitable for use on roofs within their area. Typical of this approach is the green roof on the National Weather Centre. This is a project collaboration between the University of Oklahoma Colleges of Atmospheric and Geographic Sciences and Architecture; Oklahoma Water Resource Board and the Oklahoma Conservation Commission. A 1,280ft^2 roof on the sixth floor of the National Weather Centre has been turned green, and scientific instruments are being used to track its progress. A two-year green roof study at the University of Minneapolis set out to develop guidelines for low maintenance plants that could survive the cold and dry weather conditions of the area, while reducing a building's heating costs. A variety of grasses, bulbs and perennials were trialled on the roof of the University's Williamson Hall, resulting in a list of approved plants being created which form part of the city green roof guide.

Construction of the Target Center green roof underway. (Design: Kestrel Design Group, Inspect and Leo A. Daly; Photo: Bergerson Photography)

Green roofs have only just begun to be introduced into Alaska. In 2010, the first green roof in the state was installed at the Downtown Transportation Center, Juneau. Planting was deliberately designed to include artistic and cultural aspects, using both sedums and native plants. Each side of the roof is designed in the style of Tingit patterns found in basketry that tell stories appropriate to the Juneau setting. About 1,000ft^2 of the roof is covered with trays of sedums and native Alaskan sea thrift. One side with red and yellow sedums represents water and tides, reflecting the proximity of the Gastinau Channel shoreline. The other side of the roof is planted with red sedums and sea thrift, representing the shaman or chief denoting that this area was once a boundary marker to Indian tribes. The roof is not accessible to the public but can be seen from overlooking buildings.

Incentive programmes are designed to reflect local needs. Portland, Oregon and Seattle have programmes offering planning incentives offering greater floor space for developments possessing green roofs. Water quality is cited as the main reason, as this is an area experiencing very high rainfall with stormwater run-off from buildings and flooding causing problems. Green roofs are promoted as a way of flood reduction. In 2010, rebates of up to $5 per square foot were being offered to anyone constructing a new green roof in Portland and Seattle. Portland's programme covers a variety of incentives and policies via different schemes, for example:

- Grey to Green initiative – provides grants helping to pay for eco-roof construction.
- Green Building Policy – relates to city owned buildings. Whenever an existing city owned building is given a new roof or a new building is constructed, 70 per cent of the roof has to be covered with an eco-roof. The remaining 30 per cent has to be covered with reflective materials.
- Floor Area ratio bonus – relates to downtown areas and allows developers to build bigger buildings than otherwise allowed providing the building contains an eco-roof.
- Stormwater management – if an eco-roof is used, then developers can obtain reductions on other stormwater management facilities.
- Clean River Rewards programme – tax reductions are available on utility fees if stormwater is properly managed.

A research study carried out in Portland indicated that a 40,000ft^2 green roof would cost $128,803 over a five year period, but would save the building owner $403,632 over a 40 year period. In Washington developers can apply for subsidies from District initiatives such as those offered by the Neighbourhood Investment Fund available from the Deputy Mayor's Office of Planning and Economic Development. One organization that took advantage of such subsidies was the General Scott Condominiums which have impressive views of the White House, the Washington National Cathedral and the Washington Monument. The presence of a green roof has made the top of the building a community destination – users have to be persuaded to leave when access closes at 11pm.

Many public buildings and organizations are using green roofs as a way of improving energy savings. The US Postal Service is a good example of this. Its Morgan mail processing facility in Manhattan incorporates a 2.5 acre green roof. Within a year, the roof is matching the UPS energy saving estimates. Polluted stormwater run-off has reduced by 75 per cent in the summer, and 40 per cent in the winter, while energy use overall has reduced by 40 per cent. Tom Samra, vice president of facilities, says, 'The Postal Service projected the green roof would help the Morgan facility save $30,000 in annual energy expenses. We're pleased to have surpassed that goal, saving more than $1 million since the implementation of the green roof and other energy-saving measures at Morgan.'

Design elements too are coming into focus. The Minneapolis Central Library has installed a green roof designed to link local cultural and natural patterns with the influence of the Mississippi River. The river is shown by waves created across plants of varying heights with twenty to thirty species in each grouping. The wave patterns change on a seasonal basis, with different waves becoming more apparent at different times of the year depending on which species are in bloom starting with a purple and pink burst of colour as flowering moves from west to east across the roof area. A 7,500 gallon cistern system was required to collect, store and distribute rainwater for use on the vegetation. To take another example a library building at Fallbrook, San Diego County has a 3,300ft^2 green roof with a depth of about four inches. It has been estimated to weigh between 18 and 22lb per square foot. The area has been planted up using sedums to create a design around the theme of tree roots, reflecting the area's agricultural history with a symbolic root design. It has been described as garden embroidery at its finest, using shades of yellow, gold, red and pink. The plants are placed in 500 special panelled areas.

At Elmwood Park Zoo, in Montgomery County a new pavilion entitled Canopy Gardens has been built with an extensive vegetative roof designed to capture up to 70 per cent of the rainfall which would otherwise flow into the river. About 3,200ft^2 of soil has been restored enabling the green roof to replace land that was previously used by tents and buildings. The roof has approximately three inches of growing medium covered with a patchwork of species comprising an ecosystem replicating the plant kingdom in the Arctic tundra. Seven different varieties of sedum made up of 6,000 individual plants grow on the roof.

America is also leading the way in the development of professional green roof qualifications. In 2009, the Green Roof Professional Accreditation was launched. The training is delivered in individual modules or as an intensive programme. All Green Roof Professionals are required to score very highly on a multi-disciplinary exam that is offered in different cities across North America. Green Roofs for Healthy Cities requires anyone who achieves the qualifications to participate in continuing education courses to improve their green roof expertise and maintain their accreditation. Advanced courses include subjects like urban rooftop agriculture, integrated water management and green walls.

Looking at developments worldwide, it is clear that the growth of green roofs at both consumer and business levels have been greatest where there are financial and legislative incentives. Cities like Toronto, Portland, Oregon, Chicago and Linz have seen the numbers of green roofs grow substantially as a result. When financial and legislative incentives are combined with active government participation, cities can become green very quickly.

Signs too exist of a move towards expanding the usage of roofs away from just passive provision towards opening up roofs for greater amenity use or turning them into food growing areas.

5 HOW TO CHOOSE AND INSTALL A GREEN ROOF

Having decided in favour of a green roof, the next step is to choose and install it. Bear in mind that DIY installations are best used for small projects such as sheds, pergolas, dog kennels. Anything that requires financing via a mortgage or is linked to an existing property such as a garage should be left to a recognized contractor. Mortgage and bank lenders will require warranties on all roofing work, as with any major construction project. Such warranties will only be provided by recognized contractors – you cannot get them for DIY work.

Start by deciding what style is required. Is it to be an intensive green roof similar to an ordinary garden complete with trees, planters, and shrubs? Or is the preference for an extensive low-growing roof of sedums, wildflowers and other long-lived perennials? Will access be required regularly or can the garden simply be admired from a distance? How important are environmental considerations, dealing with stormwater, water saving or energy usage?

Check if planning permission is required. For all large buildings, this will be mandatory. For smaller domestic roofs on garages or houses, it may or may not be required depending on size and the planning requirements of local councils. For very small areas such as a dog kennel or pergola, it is unlikely that planning permission would be needed. Any garden buildings may require it, especially if they are in sight of other gardens. If there is any doubt, it is always best to check with your local authority before commencing work.

If planning permission is required, it may mean that the planning authorities will have requirements as to biodiversity and environmental considerations that have to be met in the final scheme.

OPPOSITE: This green roof over the National Trust's public toilets at Kynance Cove, Cornwall, was designed to blend in to the landscape. Difficult to spot, it is the turfed area behind the white building.

COMPONENTS

It is not enough to simply put a waterproof layer, soil and plants on the roof. To be successful, a green roof needs more than that. All green roofs, whether extensive or intensive in design, share the same basic components:

- An original roof floor
- Waterproof membrane
- Root protection membrane
- Drainage membranes
- Growing medium
- Planting
- Landscaping.

CONSTRUCTION

The amount of work involved depends on whether you are retrofitting a green roof to an existing building, or incorporating it into a new building. Most small projects will involve a retrofit and will probably require the building to be strengthened so as to carry the extra weight of soil and plants – particularly when wet.

A wooden or metal framework built around the existing roof will hold the roofing materials in place, but it will need extra support from posts underneath. Once the framework is in place, the roof surface needs to be covered with a thick layer

Barrel-style green roof. (Photo: Karis Youngman)

Green roof layers being built up.

Green roof layers in place.

Installation of a large extensive green roof in progress. (Photo: Adnams)

of waterproofing. This is followed by a root barrier membrane, drainage layer, a water retention mat and finally the sedum matting, turf or soil and chosen vegetation.

COSTS

The cost of installing a green roof will depend entirely on the size of the project and the style of roof that is being installed. Small DIY projects can be relatively inexpensive; the cost is increased substantially according to the size of the roof and whether a contractor is used. Installing sedum or wildflower matting will be more expensive than using plugs and growing your own plants. Bridget and Michael, builders of the Eco-Shed in Potter Heigham managed to keep the cost of a green roof over their 60m^2 shed down to £250 by looking for inexpensive materials, growing their own plants and doing everything themselves.

The most cost effective way of installing a roof garden or green roof is when the roof needs to be replaced or is newly constructed. Work on the basis that, on average, a green roof will cost about 50 per cent more than a conventional roof. The construction budget has to include any possible structural or safety requirements, waterproofing, membranes, irrigation systems, garden materials, maintenance costs, transport and any costs relating to obtaining planning permission. It is important to set against this the fact that long-term costs can make a significant difference. A green roof can increase the lifespan of the roof by about 50 per cent because it protects surfaces from degradation by the sun and harsh weather.

Grants may be available from various sources such as development programmes. Such grants depend entirely on local conditions, and are usually only available for businesses, public amenities or large projects. It is very unlikely that you would get funding assistance to put a green roof on areas such as a dog kennel or a shed. In some countries tax subsidies on water or local authority rates may be available once the green roof is complete.

When comparing costs of a green roof to a conventional roof, you need to take into account not just the initial construction costs, but other related costs such as maintenance. Then against the costs, you need to consider the effect on energy consumption and energy bills over several (at least ten) years.

ACCESS

This is extremely important and should be considered at the very beginning of any project. Whatever the height of the building, you do have to be able to cope with this factor. There is no use putting a green roof on a building if you are going to get dizzy and run the risk of falling every time you go up to maintain or use it! The roof has to be easily accessible. You have to work out from the beginning just how materials are going to be taken onto the roof. The materials can be extremely heavy – too heavy to simply carry up a ladder over your shoulder or in your hand. Pieces of sedum matting can weigh up to 80Kg to get up onto the roof – a forklift truck may be needed, as well as fall restraints to protect you when working on the roof. Even if you are only covering a small area such as a summerhouse or birdhouse, several pairs of hands will be needed to hold the matting and secure the ladders. Electrical points may be required when using drills or other mechanical equipment.

Long-term maintenance – weeding, fertilizing, clearing drains – will also require safe access. Depending on the height of the building, ladders may not be enough. Scaffolding or platforms may be required or it may be possible to use interior staircases or lifts.

Unless the project is very tiny and immediately accessible, it will require people to stand and move about on the roof. This means that the basic structure of the roof has to be sound, and strong.

PITCH

The pitch of the roof will determine what type of roof you can consider. An intensive roof garden has to be either flat or have a maximum sloping pitch of 5 degrees whereas an extensive green roof can be installed on roofs with a slope of up to 45

This is a good example of two steeply-sloping roofs, the larger of which covers 250 m^2. (Photo: Ulrik Reeh Veg Tech)

degrees. Roofs that slope at an angle of more than 22 degrees will need supports to prevent the planting material sliding away. On steep roofs, thin mats of synthetic material or coir fibre can be used to support the growth of grasses and succulents. No gutters should be discharging directly onto the roof, otherwise the plants will be over watered.

Modern technology allows green roofs to be installed on saddle roofs, shed roofs and barrel roofs as well as traditional flat and slight pitched roofs.

LOAD BEARING

This is another very important factor that has to be borne in mind before a roof is even built. A green roof of any kind is much heavier than a traditional flat or pitched roof due to the weight of the planting material. An average saturated extensive green roof can weigh up to110Kg per square metre – this is very heavy and the roof has to be able to cope with the weight.

Intensive installations in planters or across the whole roof can vary substantially depending on

A QUICK GUIDE TO LOAD BEARING

The expected structural loading (when fully saturated) for various types of roof is as follows.

Gravel surface	90–150kg per sq m
Paving slabs	160–220kg per sq m
Extensive green roof (sedum)	60–90kg per sq m
Extensive green roof (substrate & other plants)	80–150kg per sq m
Intensive green roof	200–1000+ kg per sq m

what plants are chosen. It is usually tree pits that push up the maximum loading on a roof, but for simple turf and low-growing shrub installation 300kg would be a good starting point for minimum design load.

The bigger the roof, the greater the load capacity needed. Large commercial roofs or roofs across blocks of flats may even require machinery to move and install materials.

Water kept in tanks on the roof will add extra weight – on average about 8lb to the gallon. Adding logs, sand berms and rock piles adds further weight.

No matter what the size of the project, it is important to make sure that the roof is strong enough before you start work. If you are planning to put a green roof on a shed or kennel for example, you need to make sure that the walls and roof are thick enough to bear the weight. A cheap wooden shed from a DIY store is unlikely to be strong enough.

On larger projects, an architect or structural engineer will be required to work out the load capacity depending on use and access. Attention needs to be paid to where structures like planters and deeper planting areas will be situated as this can affect the scope of the roof structure itself. By placing such structures in the right areas, it can reduce the need for any structural reinforcement.

WIND RESISTANCE

The taller the building, the greater the problem posed by wind. The speed of the wind as it passes over a roof increases, and it can also cause wind scour – the physical movement of soil and plants. The wind chill factor can lower temperatures on roofs in wintertime and make it harder for plants to survive. On any roof, the effects of wind are always felt strongest at the corners as the wind whirls and swirls when it hits corners. This creates uplift and encourages items to move off roofs. As a result, all materials should be fastened down securely and consideration given to additional ballast in the shape of stones or gravel.

WATERPROOFING

No one wants a leaky roof, so waterproofing has to be undertaken very carefully. Waterproof membranes are usually made out of bituminous fabrics, butyl rubber and plastic. They can be used on concrete, metal, timber or plastic surfaces. For small projects, a pond liner is a good option. Ensure that all overlapping edges are fully sealed. Leaks can occur if this is not done. Michael Thompson, creator of the Eco-Shed in Norfolk, discovered this the hard way when he had to take up part of the roof after it was

Interior of a roof, with the waterproofing layers visible at the edges. (Photo: Karis Youngman)

completed, in order to deal with a leak. It had been caused by a poor overlapping join in the builder's plastic that acted as the waterproofing layer.

When the waterproof membrane has been installed, the next step must be to carry out a leak test. No one wants to plant up a roof and then find soon afterwards that leaks are appearing. Quite apart from the dangers to electrical supplies within the building, the presence of a leak can mean a lot of extra hard work having to be done on the roof. Create a temporary dam at the lowest end of the slope, or cover over drainage holes on a flat roof. Then, flood the surface with water using a hosepipe. Leave the water on the surface for twenty-four hours. Carefully watch the underneath of the roof to see if any leaks begin to emerge; they will show up and can be fixed immediately. If the roof is fully sealed and leak proof, it is less likely that problems will occur in the future. The various additional membranes and plants covering the waterproof membrane prevents any degradation by UV light. The only other risk is from sharp objects or deep-rooted plants.

ROOT PROTECTION

The waterproof membrane needs to be protected against root penetration and mechanical damage, particularly on intensive roofs where there is regular access or tall plants growing. Root protection membranes meet this need. The root barrier should be placed immediately above the drainage level. This prevents any plants with a tap root such as tree seedlings or dandelions from establishing themselves.

DRAINAGE LAYER

This usually consists of a purpose-made corrugated or moulded mat which is placed under the planting substrate.

GROWING MEDIUM

The type and amount of growing medium depends entirely on the type of vegetation you are planning. Soil depths can range from 200 to 2,000mm (8 to 80in). Extensive green roofs based on sedums, mosses and wildflowers will require a shallow soil of 200mm (8in) or less.

Intensive roofs on which shrubs and small trees will be growing require a minimum soil depth of 500mm to 600mm (20 to 24in). Larger trees will require 800 to 1300mm (32 to 50in).

The content of the growing medium, or planting substrate as it is sometimes described, has to give air and water retention plus being suitable for root growth and anchoring plants in the soil. Aggregates such as crushed brick and concrete mix, sand, gravel, peat, bark, leaf mould, coir and

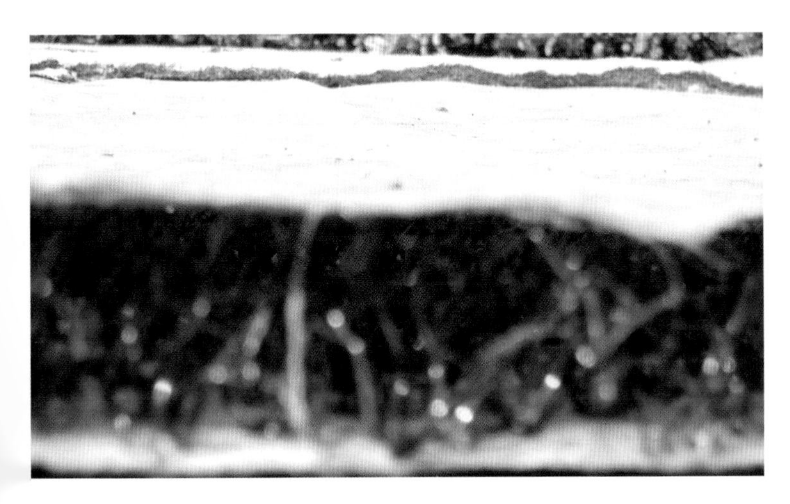

Drainage layers.

top soil have been used. Barriers should be provided to ensure that the growing medium does not block drains or drainage layers. If specific habitats are to be created on a bio-diverse roof, specialist advice should be sought with regard to soil and substrate as well as vegetation.

Sedum plugs ready for planting. (Photo: Blackdown Horticultural Consultants)

IRRIGATION

Any planned irrigation systems should be added at this stage. Such systems generally comprise porous pipes (pipes with tiny drainage holes), which are spread across the roof and covered with the growing medium.

PLANTING

Choose what type of plants you want on the roof – native wildflowers, sedum and turf are the usual options for an extensive roof, while an intensive roof can have almost any type of planting as long as the roof is strong enough to bear it.

If choosing a sedum roof, the choice is between using sedum plugs, sedum matting or raising lots of young plants from cuttings. Sedum matting is grown on an industrial scale on farms. Seed is sown onto matting placed in fields, and left to grow. When required, the matting is cut up into strips or mats ready for delivery.

Planting up a roof for use by honey bees. (Photo: Jorg Breuning/Green Roof Services LLC)

Newly-sown sedum in fields in Norfolk.

Sedum ready for harvesting in Norfolk.

Harvesting begins.

When planting a green roof, always start at the furthest side from your access points. Work backwards so that there is no need to tread on seeds, plants or sedum matting. Water in thoroughly. Fertilizer should be applied to encourage growth.

If sedum matting is being used, it is important not to leave the matting rolled up. If it is not being used immediately, the matting should be unrolled and left. If this is not done, there is a risk that the plants could die.

Metal edging holding in sedum matting.

Alternative planting methods are being introduced, particularly for larger projects. These may comprise pre-planted plastic containers that can be fitted onto the roof, or pocket bags made from recycled fibres. Pockets look set to be a popular option as they can be used to create a sculptured biodiverse habitat. They can be used to form different levels thus mimicking the natural living conditions of plants and aiding seed germination by providing shade and shelter from the wind while offering a large open area for maximum exposure to the sun. They are installed with plants already well grown, thus giving an instant vegetated space. The pockets can be linked together to form a continuous green surface, which can be easily moved when necessary for roof maintenance.

In the United States, self-contained portable blocks of green roofing are frequently supplied by contractors. These blocks can be arranged and rearranged as the owner of the roof requires. Each unit consists of a 24 × 24in container made of high-grade anodized aluminium filled with sedums.

Biodiversity can be encouraged by adding bird boxes and log piles for the wildlife to use on the roof.

Soffits holding the green roof in place.

EDGING

Make sure that the roof edging is slightly higher than the surface of the roof. This will ensure that the growing material is kept in place. Typical edgings are made of wood or metal.

The shed roof before commencement of work. (Photo: Red Rose Forest/Outerspace Landscapes)

DIY ROOFS

Keen gardeners intent on a small project can create their own tailor-made schemes. Journalist Jean Vernon retrofitted a green roof on a shed in her garden. Recognizing that the shed was not strong enough to support a green roof; she set out to strengthen it. Her solution was to remove the windows and place the shed under a separate green roof canopy, which extended outwards from the building. Heavy-duty timber posts, cross beams and strong plywood were used to create the platform. This was then covered with a damp-proof membrane, a water-retention mat and a sedum roof. To hold the sedum in place round the open edge of the roof, she used chicken wire folded over and secured into the plywood.

To take another example, Michael Thompson built a rammed earth eco-shed and constructed his own version of a green roof on top. With the aim of keeping costs to an absolute minimum,

The front view of the shed before work begins. (Photo: Red Rose Forest/Outerspace Landscapes)

ABOVE: The front view of the shed after the green roof is added. (Photo: Red Rose Forest/Outerspace Landscapes)

BELOW: The Nephra herb and sedum mix green roof. (Photo: Red Rose Forest/Outerspace Landscapes)

FACTORS TO CONSIDER WHEN DESIGNING A GREEN ROOF

- What type of green roof is required? Intensive, semi-intensive, extensive?
- If extensive, do you want wildflowers, sedums or turf?
- What substrates are to be used?
- Do you want to incorporate other features such as log piles and bird boxes to encourage bio-diversity?
- Can the roof support the weight or is additional strengthening needed?
- Can any of the surplus water drainage be reused?

builder's plastic was used to provide a waterproofing layer while top soil removed during the construction phase was reused on the roof. Plants were grown from seed and cuttings and held in place by a wooden soffit placed around the edge of the roof.

These illustrations show how a project was developed from start to finish. The project involved putting a mini-garden onto an allotment shed in Greater Manchester. Having checked the load-bearing capability of the shed, a pine frame was added, together with pond liner, root barrier and filter fleece. Vegetation was planted into a growing medium of clay aggregate, horticultural grit sand, sterilized loam and peat-free compost.

To be successful, such schemes need to be well thought out in advance with careful attention paid to making sure the roof is strong enough to hold the weight of vegetation. It can work out quite cheaply for small projects.

INSURANCE

Insurance companies are only just getting to grips with green buildings and alternative energy. Attitudes vary by country, by insurer and by individual underwriter. Before you begin any work or agree to that work, you must contact your insurer. You need to explain what you plan to do. If you are amending an existing building, there will usually be restricted cover during the construction period. For anything other than a minor home project, you should consult with a professional commercial insurance broker. The insurer will need to know about all the work you are undertaking including green roof, solar panels and wind turbines. If you do not get advance written agreement from your insurer you may find that all cover on the building is void, not just the green roof area.

6 MAINTENANCE REQUIREMENTS

No roof, whether green, brown, white, blue or conventional, is ever totally maintenance-free. Work is always needed to keep any roof in good condition. Leaks, wind or storm damage can occur to any roof. It is not possible to simply put a roof on a building of any kind and then leave it to its own devices.

Any roof that is not maintained properly will ultimately cause problems. Strategies for maintaining a roof, no matter what size it is, have to be in place from the very beginning – and this is all too forgotten when people and organizations are focusing on the benefits of having a green roof. A green roof cannot be ignored and left untouched. Even if a green roof is described as low maintenance – it does not mean there is no maintenance necessary.

ACCESS

This is the first priority when considering maintenance. How are you going to reach the roof? A small project where you can reach the roof by ladder is one thing – working on a house roof, or across a domed roof of a school or industrial building – is quite another matter. Access needs to be built in from the very beginning. Stairs, outside flights of steps may be available. Ladders should be fixed in place, or held securely while being used. A tall movable platform such as that used for cutting hedges may be sufficient, but otherwise you need to think of methods of reaching the top of a roof and coming down while checking all its aspects. Safety harnesses will be needed. Falling from a roof can cause serious or mortal injury.

ABOVE: Sedum roof requiring fertilizer and reseeding.

OPPOSITE: This green roof at Regents Place in London is carefully designed and requires careful maintenance to sustain its biodiversity. (Photo: Alumasc)

Ladder access to the green roof.

Fallnet safety systems in use. (Photo: Alumasc)

It is not unknown for people to have to abseil down a large roof in order to carry out maintenance – and this is not a task for beginners. Personal safety equipment should be used wherever risks cannot be avoided or limited by railing barriers. For example, green roof manufacturers, ZinCo offer a variety of safety systems such as Fallnet®SR rail system. This allows users to attach themselves to a fixing point that moves horizontally along the roof. The runner slides along the rails on rollers, following the user wherever they go on the roof. Alternatively, there is a grid system that can be plugged together to match the style of the roof. Users fix themselves onto the centre of the grid elements to hold themselves in place. Such systems can be retrofitted onto existing green roofs.

In the UK, the Health and Safety Executive advise that it may not be reasonably practicable to provide edge protection during short-term work. In such cases anyone working nearer than 2 metres to any unguarded edge should be using a safety harness. Where safety harnesses are used, they need to be:

- Appropriate for the user and in good condition. Full harnesses are essential, safety belts are not sufficient.
- Securely attached to an anchorage point of sufficient strength.
- Fitting as short a lanyard as possible that enables wearers to do their work.
- Actually used – tight management discipline is needed to ensure this.

Railings can be attached to flat roofs or rooftop terraces without needing to penetrate the roof covering.

Care also has to be taken to ensure that there is a safe way of removing containers full of plant debris or adding new plants and planting material onto the roof. No one wants to simply drop a full bucket from a roof – the damage and mess can be considerable, as well as the inherent risk to anyone underneath. Remember too, that such loads are always heavier than you might think – trying to climb down a ladder with a heavy bucket is neither easy nor safe.

COMMERCIAL ROOFS

Large commercial roofs are installed by specialized contractors who include a maintenance agreement, usually for a two year period, within the contract agreement. The problem of maintenance normally occurs when such contracts end. Companies should either negotiate a new rolling maintenance agreement with the original landscape company, or arrange for someone else to do it. Maintenance of a green roof should not be left to the care of the building maintenance staff – they do not have the skill or expertise that is necessary to deal with or recognize problems when they occur. Any contract agreement should take account of the specific features of the roof, its size, pitch, location, accessibility, vegetation type. It will normally be assessed at a rate per square metre per visit.

The bigger the roof, the more work required to keep it in good condition. The Park and Ride facilities at Munich Trade Fair building incorporate an 8,700m^2 lawn roof. It has a pitch ranging from 6.5 per cent to 17 per cent. The lawn requires regular mowing – this is undertaken by solar-powered robot mowers which are continuously mowing the roof area. This enables the grass to be kept at the same height.

GREEN ROOF MAINTENANCE PROGRAMME

Whatever the size of the green roof, the basic maintenance programme is always the same. All checks on materials and planting should be undertaken twice a year, once in spring, once in autumn/winter. It is useful to have a plan of the roof marked with co-ordinates so that the findings of your inspection can be clearly recorded if problems are found. This will provide a long-term record of the per-formance of the roof and help to identify the development of major problems at a very early stage.

Materials Programme

- Remove the lids of all inspection chambers and check these are in good condition.
- Ensure roof outlets and drainage/watering equipment is in good condition. Drains and gutters on a green roof have to be inspected and cleared more frequently than on a conventional roof since the risk of plant material falling into the gutters is much higher. Any vegetation barriers such as gravel, which has encroached onto the drainage outlets, should be removed.

Keeping drains clear is essential. (Photo: Enviromat)

Remove any deposits or unwanted plants growing along the edges of the roof. (Photo: Enviromat)

- Remove dirt and other deposits from drains, gutters and traps. All rainwater should be able to flow freely away.
- Check that all surrounds are firmly in place and that all surface fastenings are tight. Protective metal flashings should be securely fixed in place.
- Remove any deposits in the gravel strips at the joints and borders, or among the gravel chippings.
- Check all sealants and mortar pointing for signs of degradation.
- Make sure that any new items such as railings that have been placed on the roof are securely fixed down, and that any fixings do not disturb the waterproof membranes.
- Make a note of any repairs or damaged landscaping materials to ensure that these are undertaken or replaced as soon as possible.

Planting Materials Programme

- If using planted modules check their fastenings have not been loosened by wind and weather.
- Remove any invasive or deep-rooted weeds.
- Wildflower roofs may need mowing or strimming after flowering in order to disperse the seeds and keep the fertility of the growing medium under control.
- Fallen leaves from overhanging trees or from the roof vegetation should be removed. These can affect the biodiversity of the roof, and kill roof plants.

IRRIGATION

During the summer, many green roofs may require some form of irrigation. Roofs are exposed to higher wind levels than at ground level, and wind increases the process of evaporation thus allowing vegetation to dry out quickly. Periods of drought will also have a noticeable effect. The condition of vegetation on all types of roofs will need checking.

Intensive Roofs

Roofs covered with garden type planting will undoubtedly need much more irrigation than any other type. An automatic watering system is generally recommended such as a porous pipe system allowing water to trickle out to the roots of plants when needed.

Extensive Roofs

Sedum and other drought-resistant plants will be needed in severe droughts. Such plants have fleshy, succulent leaves that are designed to withstand

Here leaf removal is required. (Photo: Galen Youngman)

drought conditions but even they can suffer in extreme conditions. It is important to regularly check the condition of the plants to make sure they are not going wrinkly and dry. If the leaves are fleshly, then they are surviving well. If watering is needed, small areas can be undertaken with a hosepipe if there is suitable access. On larger schemes, consideration should be given to installing a porous pipe system during construction so as to be able to deal with irrigation problems when they occur. Test programmes are underway in areas where drought is common, such as the desert regions of America, to investigate the best forms of irrigation. The use of grey water has been mooted – this is water that has been used for washing hands, laundry or cooking. Middlesex University is trialling a system which involves a channel enabling grey water to flow through a collection of low-growing native plants.

Grass roofs will turn brown in summer, especially during hot periods. As with lawns on the ground, it is generally accepted that the best practice is to simply leave the grass alone and it will renew itself automatically when the rains eventually come.

Irrigation systems are generally recommended for roofs with a pitch of more than 10 degrees or south-facing roofs with a pitch of 5 degrees or more. Any windy or exposed sites are also advised to install an irrigation system. It is best to water at dawn or dusk so as to minimize unnecessary evaporation. Sedum roofs will generally require watering every four to six days during periods of extreme heat or if the plants are suffering badly.

Fertilizer

Intensive roofs – the plants will need feeding regularly just as in any garden.

Extensive roofs – in general, these roofs only need fertilizer to be applied once a year in order to keep the vegetation in good condition.

VEGETATION

The amount of plant maintenance that is required does depend entirely on the type of plants used on the roof.

Lawn edging on the green roof of a Celebrity Cruise liner. (Photo: Jorg Breuning/Green Roof Services LLG)

Turf roofs will require cutting from time to time, while grass roofs used as lawns will require normal lawn cutting procedures.

Intensive gardens with shrubs, perennials, trees or vegetables will need regular plant maintenance. Dividing plants, pruning, sowing and deadheading will have to be carried out at regular intervals. Vegetables and fruit will need to be picked. The stability of taller plants will have to be checked during windy conditions.

Extensive roofs covered in sedum, wildflowers, mosses or grass require less attention. In general, these plants tend to be self-sustaining.

Sedum roof showing signs of dryness and requiring re-seeding.

Sedum survives extreme weather conditions. It is used on buildings in America where low winter temperatures are normal. Even in the UK, where there were extremely low temperatures during the winter of 2009/2010, sedums survived in good condition. The varieties used by companies like Enviromat are extremely hardy. The major problem that was recorded during this period was linked to property maintenance. The owner had failed to remove leaves from the roof after the autumn leaf fall, and these had been left on the sedum plants. The leaves had blocked light and killed the sedum.

Sedums require feeding in spring and any dead growth removed. Seed or pieces of sedum can be sprinkled onto any bare patches of earth that have appeared. Add some water and fertilizer and leave to grow. Remove any weeds that have taken root.

A further tidy up should take place later in the year during the autumn or early winter. As in the spring check up, this should involve removing fallen leaves, any weeds or invasive plants that have taken root such as tree saplings.

Biodiversity wildflower roofs need mowing, and any checking to ensure bare patches have not appeared. New seed should be sown wherever necessary.Invasive plants such as couch grass, or deep-rooted tree saplings should be removed otherwise they may damage the waterproof membranes. If these plants are not maintained, the ecological value of the roofs will be reduced.

Always bear in mind that the appearance of an extensive green roof will change from season to season. It will not always look green. In spring and summer, sedum species will flower at different times. Weather conditions may mean faster or

Damage by rabbits.

slower growth. In the winter, sedum plants will appear to shrink back as the leaves become smaller and turn reddish brown. This merely reflects the way in which the plants are preparing for winter temperatures. Mosses may become more apparent in the winter, reflecting higher rainfall periods; and dying off during periods of summer dryness. The position of the roof and the amount of sunshine or shade it experiences at different times of the year will also affect the appearance of the vegetation.

PESTS AND DISEASES

Diseased plants should be removed and replaced during the regular checks on vegetation.

Pests such as pigeons, mice and rats can prove a problem that can be difficult to deal with, particularly if you have a biodiverse roof. Using poison could mean harming birds using the roof as a hunting area. Discussions should be held with pest control organizations as to the best means of dealing with the situation.

If a roof leads directly to the ground (as at Ralph's Place – see Chapter 7), there can be problems with rabbits trying to dig under the matting.

PUBLIC ACCESS

Any roof that has frequent public access does require some means by which litter can be collected and removed.

There is also the problem posed by smokers. Commercial buildings normally have a non-smoking policy. This means that smokers go outside for a smoke. If there is access to the roof, many smokers will use this. Cigarettes and sparks can be a hazard to dry grass and vegetation. As a result, consideration should be made to making roof gardens smoke-free areas.

Work On Adjoining Roof Areas

If work is taking place on any adjoining roof areas, always take care that the green roof construction is not damaged in any way.

7 CASE STUDIES

COB BALE HOUSE, BANHAM, NORFOLK, UK

The Cob Bale House was designed and built by Kate Edwards in 2007 and is used as a private studio for workshops and meditation. The green roof is regarded as an integral part of the overall sustainability of the project.

Cob is formed from a mixture of sandy subsoil, clay and straw. It is a traditional building material, which has been used for thousands of years worldwide. The walls are very strong and good for load bearing. It also possesses good thermal mass qualities, absorbing heat during the day and releasing it slowly during the night. This makes it a good fit with the benefits of a green roof.

The Cob Bale House is built as a roundhouse and is 22ft in diameter. It is carefully orientated to maximize solar gain. Cob and glass are used on the south-facing walls, while the north-facing walls are a mixture of straw bales and cob so as to maximize insulation. The cob walls and floor were made using only sand and clay from the site. Straw bales came from surrounding farms, and are held together with hazel twigs cut from local trees. The walls are two feet thick. It took around four months to build and cost £30,000.

The roof has a 30 degree pitch. It was constructed using English Oak and Douglas Fir for the rafters and the edging. The rafters were then covered with boards, plastic garden liner, root protection membrane, cardboard and old carpet; followed by soil and turf sods. The turf roof did not last long. The owner found it difficult to maintain and consequently, it was replaced with sedum plugs. Up to 300 plugs were used to cover the roof at a rate of eight per square metre. The sedums took root quickly and soon covered the entire roof.

RIGHT: View of Cob Bale roundhouse with its sedum roof. (Photo: Karis Youngman)

OPPOSITE: Golf clubhouse with green roof. (Photo: Alumasc)

The roundhouse in autumn, showing its original turf roof. (Photo: Kate Edwards)

Interior view of the roundhouse roof. (Photo: Karis Youngman)

ECO-SHED, POTTER HEIGHAM, NORFOLK, UK

Located at Potter Heigham on the Norfolk Broads, the Eco-Shed is an innovative DIY project. The owner, Michael Thompson, set out to create a shed which would be as sustainable as possible, and to keep the cost to an absolute minimum. 'We aimed for a shed for £1 or as little as possible,' said Michael Thompson.

The single-storey, $60m^2$ building was designed and built by Michael Thompson, after watching a programme on rammed earth buildings. As a carpenter by trade, he needed work space as well as garden shed facilities. With plans to redevelop the garden, he began work on the shed as the first priority. In order to make maximum use of space, the shed is situated against one of the boundary lines with a neighbouring property and is built in the shape of a grand piano. Michael taught himself to use rammed earth building techniques and now runs regular courses on the subject.

> Rammed earth has a long history, it was used on the Great Wall of China. It is a 9,000-year-old technology. I wanted to do a curved building. We used a concrete base. 66 per cent of the earth came from the garden as we excavated the foundations. We kept the top soil separate for use on the roof. The sub-soil was used to make the rammed earth blocks. There was not enough to make the walls so we brought in another 13 tons of soil from Stalham. The two soil types were blended in equal proportions and we added a small amount of cement for strength. The soil and cement were mixed in a mixer, and moisture was added to hold it together and stabilize the cement. We used blood, lime and ash. This made strong walls. The material was rammed into the moulds, already in place on the walls. Each mould was 2m long, 1m high. When the blocks were dry, the moulds were removed and set in place ready for the next layer.

Sedum roof with gravel dividers and at the far end the clover area.

Interior view of the roof showing the rafters and boards.

The roof has a pitch of 5 degrees and was constructed out of wooden rafters, strengthened by the moulds used to make the rammed earth blocks. A wooden soffit was created around the edge of the roof. Builders' plastic was used as a waterproof layer, together with root protection layers. Top soil, dug out when the foundations were constructed, was used to provide a growing medium. Over 300 buckets of soil were carried onto the roof via a network of ladders and ramps. The soil was taken up two buckets at a time and placed at the far end of the roof, moving steadily backwards as the roof was covered. The soil is about 7.5 to 10cm (3 to 4in) deep. Some stones

Clover area with log pile.

View of roof showing curved edges and the varied planting of sedums, wild flowers and clover.

were added to hold down the felting at the edges. Gravel was inserted in strips dividing up planting areas.

The green roof is mainly sedum, cultivated by his wife Bridget from soft stem cuttings. Over 400 plugs were created from two plants purchased at a cost of £5.98. The plugs have flourished and spread. Further planting has been carried out to create a bio-diverse roof attracting a wider range of insects. A packet of thyme seeds was sprinkled on the roof, and some of these have taken and grown through the sedum plants. Some wildflower plants were added but few survived. Originally there was a turf area, but this did not succeed, and has been replaced by clover, which has grown well. Despite the bitter winter of 2009/2010; the roof plants have thrived. Virginia Creeper grows up the walls.

Any rainwater that is not required by the green roof is diverted and collected into an underground storage tank. This is then piped to water barrels on the other side of the garden and used to water the owner's fruit and vegetable area.

The total cost of the shed came to £2,700, and took 2,700 hours to complete. The roof itself cost £250 and that price included a *Guide to DIY Green Roofs* by Dusty Gedge; geotextiles root protector; rolls of builders' plastic totalling around £100; and two sedum plants costing £5.98 out of which Bridget took 400 cuttings. Some packets of seed were purchased later. Michael Thompson explained:

> We would have been better using a butyl liner rather than builders' plastic but because of the shape this would have had to have been bespoke, and would have cost another £1,000. The builders' plastic will last about ten years and at that point we will have to replace it. The only problem was when we had a leak. This was not caused by the planting; it was because we had not sealed the builders' plastic correctly. The builders' plastic came in 4m wide lengths and at its widest point, the roof is 7m. We had to use overlapping layers and did not seal the overlap properly. We had assumed that the weight of the earth would seal it, but it didn't. We had to move about 2 tons of earth in order to get access to the roof to seal the leak and prevent it happening elsewhere on the roof.

Access for maintenance is via a metal ladder fastened to the wall and into the ground beside the shed. The ladder is extremely strong, having been recycled from the docks and was previously used to provide access from ships onto the dock.

THE ENTERPRISE, SPARKHOUSE, LINCOLN, UK

The Enterprise project is the second phase of development to Sparkhouse Studios located on the University of Lincoln's Brayford Pool campus, Lincoln. The Enterprise building is a four-storey structure housing the university department Enterprise@Lincoln providing dedicated space for new business growth and opportunities for entrepreneurship linking the university with local and regional businesses.

The building is located in the south-east corner of the campus adjacent to the restored old Station Master's office and is designed to reflect the idea of trains standing at the platform with overhanging pods symbolizing the form of old locomotives. As the location originally comprised contaminated railway sidings, the ecological value of the site was extremely low. The scheme had an ecologist appointed to increase species within the landscape.

The roof incorporates a PV panel array to provide renewable energy offsetting the buildings electrical energy usage, together with a mixed mat green roof.

Supplied by Sky-Garden, the mat was designed to be regionally applicable, possess a high aesthetic value and be tolerant of minimal trafficking. A mixture of plants was chosen mainly because of its aesthetic qualities. The sedum element goes brown in the winter, and the other plants can compensate for the visual element. The mixed mat requires a little more maintenance and water than a traditional sedum mat. It is drought tolerant.

Installing the mat required some care. Due to the slope of the roof, retention systems had be inserted to prevent slippage and minimize movement. Smaller amounts of materials had to be used at any one time as bulk items could not be dropped to the roof area. 40 to 50mm (1.5 to 2in) of purpose-produced sedum substrate was used – this comprised crushed brick with 10 per cent compost.

The long-term maintenance is minimal, involving just one or two visits per year to trim, weed and feed the roof.

GOATS ON THE ROOF, NORTHUMBERLAND, UK

Nina Remnant moved to Northumberland in 2007. She and her family purchased a 200 acre farm with the intention of breeding rare breed animals and also making it open to the public. In 2010, they decided to open a coffee shop so as to provide extra public facilities and encourage visitors to stay longer. As the farm is on the edge of the Northumberland National Park, it was important that the new building would blend into the countryside. The original intention was to build a log cabin with a turf roof. Then relatives visiting Canada saw a farm shop that had goats moving around on the roof. They thought this was a brilliant idea and perfect for the new coffee shop. It would be marvellous publicity and promote the ethos of the farm.

Discussions with designers and architects resulted in a decision to use a sedum rather than turf roof. Nina Remnant explained:

> When we looked at how heavy a turf roof would be and how much extra weight loading was required, we felt it needed to be changed. Sedum was chosen as the best alternative. The architects and designers also looked at the way the roof needed to be designed in order to give access to the goats and cope with them. The goats are not heavy enough to add much extra weight. Hygiene is no problem – the drainage system and soakways deal with any waste.

Planning permission took eight months to obtain. Nina believes that installing a sedum roof was definitely a selling point. 50 per cent of the cost of the roof was funded by the Rural Development programme for England. The overall cost was about £24,000 but this does not include reinforcing costs to the roof.

The coffee shop building is made of pine, in a log cabin style. The cabin was built in Finland and shipped over. Redland Roofing added a plastic membrane, drainage membranes, soil and sedums. The roof measures 23x8m and has a 1 in 8 pitched roof. Thirteen different types of sedum were used. The roof had three weeks to settle in before the goats were added.

> We chose to introduce Bagot goats. These are quite small and rare. Bagots came over in 1066 with the Normans and grow to about two to three feet tall. We have three goats and plan to increase the flock to five. We have a paddock at the back of the building with a ladder so that the goats can get onto the roof. They can climb quite well – Bagots are known to climb trees. Children love to see them on the roof. They get quite disappointed when they arrive and find the goats are in the paddock. As soon as they hear the goats' feet moving about on the roof, kids and adults dash out of the coffee shop to see the goats and take pictures. It has become very much a talking point. The cost has paid off in publicity and branding. It is a huge selling point to our business. It has aroused public interest and awareness of our coffee shop. People come just to see the goats on the roof. The building and the goats have been on You Tube. People cannot believe what they are seeing,
>
> The sedums are surviving well, but in places the goats tear up patches with their horns and roll on the sedums. We need to replace some patches. The goats tend to rough it up rather than eat it.
>
> It is a warm building. There have been periods of heavy rainfall. I feared there might be a landslide from the roof but that has not happened. It looks fantastic. Sedum blends in well with the environment and the goats are definitely popular.

KENSINGTON ROOF GARDENS, LONDON, UK

Kensington Roof Gardens are one of the oldest roof gardens in the UK situated one hundred feet above Kensington High Street in London. Built by George Hancock in 1938, it originally formed an intensive roof garden on top of the Derry & Toms department store, Kensington, London. The gardens were the idea of the vice president of Barkers of Kensington, which also owned Derry & Toms. The gardens have remained constantly in existence. In the late 1960s, House of Fraser purchased Barkers of Kensington. It closed Derry & Toms, but kept Barkers as a flagship store. Derry & Toms became a BIBA store, then a nightclub called Regines until it was purchased by Virgin Group in 1981. The Roof Gardens are now part of Virgin Limited Edition, the luxury portfolio of Virgin Hotels Group Limited.

Aerial view of the Spanish Garden within its London rooftop setting. (Photo: Kensington Roof Gardens)

After BIBA closed, there was a danger that the roof gardens would be redeveloped. Local residents obtained tree preservation orders and this ensured that the gardens had to be kept in good condition. There are now six trees on site that are over seventy years old. There is a rolling preservation order that covers all trees over 12in in diameter. The trees are regarded as individually special because they are growing six floors above the ground.

Access to the building is via Derry Street, just off Kensington High Street. The gardens are open to the public, as well as being accessible to customers of the Roof Garden restaurants. If the gardens are not booked for an event, anyone can come up to the gardens at any time. There is total open access. There are many regular visitors as well as people revisiting after seeing the gardens as children many years earlier.

The gardens were redesigned in 2008, finally reopening in 2009. Situated on the sixth floor of the building, the gardens incorporate between 600 and 1,000m^2 of heavy silt loam soil. Occupying 1.5 acres, the gardens contain over seventy full size trees. They are divided into three themed areas.

The Spanish Garden

This is based on the Alhambra in Granada, Spain and has a Moorish style. The restoration of the Spanish garden was based on images and photographs taken in 1957. These were used because there was a full set of pictures showing how the twenty-year-old gardens looked at the time. Some of the original grapevines still existed, and others were purchased to fill in the gaps. The garden is effectively a Koranic garden containing all the plants that are mentioned in the Koran such as olives, dates, figs, grapes, pomegranates and rosemary.

Tudor Garden

This is filled with evergreen shrubs surrounded by wisteria, lilies, roses and lavender during the summer. The design is based on planting that was undertaken when BIBA owned the garden. They planted a black and white garden and this has been continued with lots of black (very dark red/purple) and white roses; together with plants that would have been recognized by the Tudors: for example white lilies, white lavender, black cow parsley, *Dianthus* 'Mrs Simkins', black and white tulips, *Aquilegia* 'William Guinness', lily of the valley, myrtle and black-leaved *Sambuccus* 'Black lace'. During the winter, a marquee is placed in the garden.

English Woodland

This area contains fully-grown oak and fruit trees growing in just 1.5m of soil. There are mulberry, limes, English oaks, American redwood – all of which are 30ft tall. These are pruned on a three-yearly cycle.

Thousands of *narcissi*, crocus, *muscari* and anemones bloom each spring within the woodland giving a pastel, gentle feel to the area. There is also a flowing stream stocked with fish and wildlife including four resident flamingos – Bill, Ben, Splosh and Pecks – and resident ducks. The ducks and flamingos have clipped wings to prevent them leaving the garden.

During the restoration, the lawn areas were extended so that it is now as large as it was originally and it enabled features such as bridges, which had been lost in the ivy, to be recovered.

A team of gardeners maintain the roof gardens. Watering is undertaken by hand as this enables them to check each plant individually, and ensure that only as much water as is really needed is used. Weeding is undertaken by hand. No garden chemicals are used, and home-made compost is used to feed the plants. A greenhouse is used to propagate summer bedding. Bougainvillea is grown in pots against the walls of the Spanish garden and is moved into the greenhouse during the winter.

The gardeners are constantly trying to explore the boundaries of roof gardening, to see what might or might not survive. New plants are constantly being trialled. Wind is not a major problem as there is an eight-foot high wall around the garden. More food is being grown on the roof as a means of reducing the building's carbon footprint.

Cooking apples, 'Cox's Orange Pippin' eating apples, medlars and almonds are grown in the woodland. These provide blossom in spring, and the fruit is picked to use in the restaurant in the autumn. Other food grown includes courgettes for flower and fruit, rhubarb, chillis, asparagus, herbs, annual herbs such as basil, salad leaves of all kinds from dandelion leaves to lettuce. Cabbage, tomatoes, lettuce and dwarf beans are grown in planters outside the restaurant – diners are keen to see where their food has been growing earlier in the day.

The roof surfaces were checked when restoration took place and it was found that the areas covered by vegetation had survived extremely well. Most of the damage to the roof surface was in the areas open to the elements.

LITTLE GREEN ROOFS, MANCHESTER, UK

Little Green Roofs is a project that has been set up in Manchester, UK in an attempt to transform the roofs of small, uninhabited communal buildings and structures such as sheds, bike shelters and storage containers into havens for wildlife.

The project began in 2010. The organizers are Red Rose Forest. This is an environmental regeneration initiative and the Community Forest for central and western Greater Manchester. It set out to work with local residents, community groups and schools to deliver Little Green Roof projects across Manchester. The project is part funded by Manchester City Council's Carbon Innovation Fund.

Green roof on a water tank at St Chad's church, Manchester. (Photo: Red Rose Forest/Outerspace Landscapes)

Herb roof on top of a garden shed, New Moston. (Photo: Red Rose Forest/Outerspace Landscapes)

Toy store roof adapted for nature study at Stanley Grove Community Primary School. (Photo: Red Rose Forest/Outerspace Landscapes)

A variety of green roofs are being created. The exact type depends on the location and the organization involved. Non-organic material such as crushed brick is used to provide a porous lightweight growing medium which holds oxygen and water. This is then sown with wildflower seeds and becomes a haven for vertebrates. Alternatively, soil or compost is used on the green roof and, depending on depth used to grow a wide variety of plants, and where access is easy, herbs and vegetables. In each case, the construction of the roof is led by experts from Outerspace Landscape and Red Rose Forest, working alongside the community group. In addition, each project construction day will also act as a training workshop for environmental staff who want to learn more about building green roofs.

A toy shed roof at Stanley Grove Community Primary School was the first green roof to be installed as part of the project. The £850 mini-garden hosted wildflowers and herbs and is located at the right height for children to see it on a daily basis. Gary Constant, headmaster of Stanley Grove Primary School, said, 'This project is fantastic. Not only does our Little Green Roof brighten the place up, it also helps local nature and our environment. Children will get involved with looking after the garden. They will learn important practical lessons about wildlife, biodiversity and the impact of climate change.'

The green roof covered a 3 × 2m metal toy container and was made from a frame of pine wood, pond liner and filter fleece. The substrate growing medium comprised Leca (light expanded clay aggregate) mixed with horticultural grit sand, a small amount of sterilized loam and peat-free compost. The roof was planted up with lavender, rosemary, thyme, chives, blue fescue and *Sedum*

'Aurea'. Two small ponds were added to attract birds for bathing, and some dead wood was positioned on the roof to attract invertebrates.

In a separate project, St Peter's RC High School in Gorton installed a much larger, grass-covered roof as part of a £3.1 million extension.

Northfield's Day Centre at New Moston Greater Manchester put a mini garden on top of their allotment shed. Bren Fawcett from the resident's association NEPHRA says that it is projects like this that create community pride and stop anti-social behaviour:

> Six years ago, this wasn't a nice place at all. Kids would break windows, play football and get drunk. There was a real need for our community to come together. So we decided to get together and create a resident's association for the surrounding area. The interest from residents was huge and the idea just snowballed into more and more exciting projects. The latest addition is our Little Green Roof; it's our pride and joy. Now trouble on the site just doesn't happen. The kids see how beautiful everything, including the roof, looks and they leave it alone because they respect the time and effort we have put in and they want to keep it that way.
>
> The Little Green Roof Project is great. People are intrigued and it benefits everyone. It brought together different people including local volunteers, day centre staff, service users and Red Rose Forest staff. It was great fun and helped build friendships, confidence and community spirit. And herbs growing on the roof will be used with other vegetables grown on site to provide food for our luncheon club.

The roof cost £750 and covered a roof measuring 1.5 × 3.2m. The frame was made out of pine, covered with pond liner and filter fleece. The growing medium comprised Leca (light expanded clay aggregate) mixed with horticultural grit sand, a small amount of sterilized loam and peat-free compost. It was planted up with rosemary, thyme, chives, blue fescue and a sedum mat.

St Chad's Church, Withington Manchester installed a Little Green Roof on top of a water tank on the church roof. The project cost £850. The wooden water tank measured 2.5x1.5m. Pine was used to create a wooden frame, pond liner for waterproofing and filter fleece to protect the waterproof layer. The substrate was made of growing medium comprising Perlite mixed with horticultural grit sand, a small amount of sterilized loam, and a small amount of peat-free compost. The roof was planted with *Sedum* 'Aurea', *Sedum* 'Reflexum', blue fescue, *Festuca* sp, thyme and chives with the aim of attracting bees and invertebrates.

Kevin Wigley from Red Rose Forest says:

> These roofs really bring a community together. They become the talk of the neighbourhood, as well as providing a range of important benefits to wildlife and our environment. And this is just the beginning. We are looking for more small, uninhabited buildings where the roofs can be transformed into eye-catching new habitats. Community centres, places of worship, colleges, schools, Surestart centres, health centres – they are all eligible for the roofs.

NORTH HARRINGAY PRIMARY SCHOOL, LONDON, UK

The garden on the roof of North Harringay Primary School opened on July 9 2005. It is an inner London school. The garden was created on the roof of a school gymnasium.

The project was the result of an idea by Melissa Ronaldson of the London Community Herbalists (LCH) who had developed a long-standing relationship with the school. LCH had been working with pupils, educating them on where their food comes from and how naturally occurring plants can provide basic medicinal benefits and remedies. As there were hardly any soft surfaces available in the school grounds, growing areas were initially provided on the playground by topsoil held in check by railway sleepers. After visiting the gymnasium roof to gather up some discarded plant pots, Melissa Ronaldson had the idea of creating a roof garden that would also return 'a dead space' back to the community. LCH worked with Alumasc

Technical Services to work out the options of turning the roof into a garden including identifying the best type of growing medium and the logistics of getting all the materials onto the roof.

The roof garden was ultimately made out of Derbigum and ZinCo green roof layers, SSM45 Moisture Mat, FD25 Drainage layer with SF fitter sheet attached and Xincolit substrate mixed with local top soil. The garden was match funded by the local authority and is now used on a regular basis as part of the school curriculum for educational and community purposes.

According to the London Community Herbalists:

The international roof garden at North Harringay Primary School uses sustainable building technologies, and features plants that can be used for food and for medicine. Our plants, the atmosphere and aim of our garden is to value, and celebrate the rich cultural diversity, knowledge and tradition of our local area.

RALPH'S PLACE, PLUMSTEAD, NORFOLK, UK

Owner George Owen built Ralph's Place in 2001. The site was a rural location, adjacent to wood-

An unloved gymnasium roof at North Harringay Primary School has become a wildlife and vegetable haven for school use. (Photo: Alumasc)

The sloping roof design of Ralph's Place. (Photo: Galen Youngman)

The sloping sides of the sedum roof merge into a wild flower area.

land and open fields. There was a small prefabricated building on the site that had been originally built in the 1930s, which blended into the countryside. George Owen did not want to lose that close link with the area, and so he decided to build a timber-framed house that would blend in. The green roof can only be seen from the front of the house – at the back, the windows reach from floor to ceiling.

We lived in a caravan on the site while the house was being built. Contractors were used to undertake all the technical work, while George Owen did as much as possible himself. The roof line at the front goes right down to the ground. A Bauder system was used for the green roof, and the Bauder representative oversaw the installation. George Owen said:

> We used 65m roof boards, vapour layer, 90ml of polyurethane, two more layers of roofing felt one of which was a root protection layer, then the vegetation. We had to use a different technique to lay the sedum matting. The roof pitch is 30 degrees and is quite steep on either side. Sedum matting usually comes in 2m squares and this would not have worked on this roof. We had to have strips 10m long. We used a crane to lift the heavy rolls to the top of the house and suspended it like a spindle. The top of the roll was fixed to the roof, then we pulled the rest of the roll down to the bottom of the roof across steel cones to hold it in place. It was much heavier than even we expected. It took a day to put the roof on.

A leaky pipe system was used for the first year to ensure that the sedums gained enough water to establish on the roof. This has now been discontinued. George Owen recognizes that the top of the roof does get drier than it should do, since rainwater flows away and does not settle at the top. Maintenance is minimal. Owen adds some fertilizer once a year, and he has to remove any thistles or tree saplings that have taken root.

The biggest problem experienced at Ralph's Place has been the mix of sedums on the roof. Some have survived; others have not. Parts of the roof have been taken over by native sedum species and moss. With the house situated close to a wood, moss is very prevalent. George Owen says 'it reflects the march of nature, you can manage it but cannot stop it. What we have lost is the colour during the flowering phase, now we just have white flowers rather than a mix of colours.'

Rabbits do try and burrow underneath the matting where it reaches the ground.

Owen aimed to have a roof that blended into the environment. Ten years on, it is clear that he has succeeded. Viewed from a neighbouring field, the front of the house is hardly visible. 'It is very good camouflage and this is the biggest benefit for us. The roof harbours a lot of insects and it provides a habitat for birds and bats. On a summer evening we get a lot of bats flying about the roof because the roof is full of bugs.'

Despite being in a very rural setting, there were no objections to the design from local people. It blends inextricably into the environment. Nowadays, it is often referred to as the 'Teletubby house'.

SEDUM HOUSE, GIMINGHAM, NORFOLK, UK

Architect Tom Brown designed his own house in North Norfolk.

> We bought a plot of land from my father-in-law. It had planning permission for a chalet type

Chain-covered drain. (Photo: Karis Youngman)

Front view of the house with its barrel-shaped roof and drainage chain. (Photo: Karis Youngman)

> bungalow but we wanted to build something more in keeping with the setting. We wanted to build into the hillside and use as many natural materials as possible. The planning authorities gave us permission and we started work. We lived in caravans on site for two years. I did as much as possible myself and used contractors where necessary.

The two-storey house is built on a flat site that used to be a sand quarry. The back of the house is built into the hillside, so as to maximize insulation qualities. Bedrooms are on the ground floor in wings on either side of the main family rooms. The living room is on the first floor, giving good views across the countryside. Polystyrene blocks were used to form the structure of the house, covered with natural timber and flint from a local quarry. There is no gas or oil heating as all heating is provided by ground heat cultivated under the front lawn and brought via cables into the building. A wind turbine sits above the house.

The green roof comes in three areas. A barrel-shaped 16x6m sedum roof covers the main part of the house, and there are sedum blankets covering the slopes leading to decking over the side wings. Installation of the roof took two days and was carried out by Bauder. 'I used contractors to put the roof on. I needed an insurance-backed warranty for the roof so as to get the mortgage money. They put on all the felting and installation layers, then tested it for leaks before adding the sedum vegetation,' commented Tom Brown.

The roof pitch varies. The main part of the roof ranges from 0 to 15 degrees, but the side banks are 30 degrees. Very little maintenance is required apart from applying fertilizer once a year. On one side of the house the sedum matting has suffered badly from the activities of the family dog, who uses the decking to watch for visitors. Whenever visitors appear, the dog runs down the

Front view of Sedum House, showing the tiered roof with sedum descending down the side of the ground floor windows. (Photo: Karis Youngman)

Aerial view of Sedum House. (Photo: Karis Youngman)

bank to greet them – damaging the sedums in the process.

An innovative idea deals with roof drainage. Hanging from the front of the roof down to the ground are long lengths of chain. Tom Brown explains how it works.

> The chains act as drain posts. Water drips from chain to chain down to the soakaway under the coil of ground loops. I saw this system when I was a student on a trip to Venice, and thought it was a good idea. You can get some splattering if it is very windy as the downpipe is wider than the drain hole. It can look like a mini-waterfall in bad weather, but if there is just a short sharp shower, you cannot see anything. The only problem was when there was a sharp frost – there was a layer of ice on the coil of ground loops, which had to be broken.

SHARROW PRIMARY SCHOOL, SHEFFIELD, UK

The Biodiversity Green Roof, on the Sharrow Primary School in Sheffield, was the first green roof in the UK to achieve Nature Reserve Status. It was declared a local nature reserve in 2010. The concept has also several different awards including Civic Building of the Year.

The roof was created in 2007 with the aim of teaching children about wildlife and gardening. It occupies 2,000m^2 of roof space across three levels.

The nature reserve on top of Sharrow School, Sheffield. (Photo: Bauder)

Restrictions on available ground space opened up the opportunity to create green roofs within the school at three different levels to provide play space, 44m^2 of outdoor classrooms and a 1,200m^2 biodiversity roof designed to replicate a meadow, complete with cornflowers and other urban plants. Over 700 types of plant are involved. Planted species include yarrow, ox-eye daisy, mugwort, common ragwort, thistle, Michaelmas daisy, Oxford ragwort, coltsfoot, hawkbit, mullein, red valerian, purple toadflax, and teasel.

The biodiversity roof has been landscaped to reflect different habitats that can be found in and around the city, for example wetland, meadow, dead tree and a bird table. The wetland area comprises a small pond on the roof.

It is a haven for birds and other kinds of wildlife, with rotting tree stumps used by many types of insects. All of the roofs are used as a learning resource with curriculum-friendly uses for all the children. Children are not allowed on the top roof. There is no fence around it so it is not safe for them to use. Instead, children can look through a window onto the roof and watch the wildlife.

All the first-floor classrooms have integral terrace roof gardens. These provide small wildlife habitats where children can grow sunflowers, vegetables and other flowers. Children can also study the wildlife on the terraces.

The roof incorporates a BREEM A+ rated Bauder waterproofing system possessing 120mm of PIR insulation to achieve a U value of 0.2W/m2 constructed on a concrete deck. The roof was designed and built in-house.

Biodiversity has definitely increased as a result of the installation of the green roof. Surveys carried out by Sheffield City Ecology Service have revealed that additional plant species are appearing having colonized the roof spontaneously. The dense and varied vegetation is attracting birds and insects.

THE VENNY, AUSTRALIA

The Venny is situated in JJ Holland Park, Kensington, Victoria, Australia and is owned by the city of Melbourne. The building forms a community facility and play area. It provides facilities and programmes supporting young people in the area. In 2007, the building was condemned due to the discovery that asbestos existed in the foundations of the building. A further problem was drainage, as it had been badly designed to cope with a flood plain situation.

The decision was taken to redevelop The Venny, moving it to a new site above the flood plain. A larger facility was to be created which would include a multi-purpose room, kitchen, laundry, storage area, offices, outdoor covered-deck and a flexible play area. Budget restrictions forced them to look closely at the actual construction of the building and it was decided to convert some disused shipping containers. These would be strong, secure and link into the landscape – the site was near the port. However, using shipping containers did bring problems. The metal kept the heat in the building, the interiors were very noisy and the roof was vulnerable to rust due to the presence of standing water. A green roof was chosen as the solution since the presence of vegetation would reduce heat, protect the steel containers, improve storm water drainage and reduce noise.

A two-year research project was set up to investigate what type of green roof would be best for the site. This research formed a collaboration between the City of Melbourne and the University of Melbourne's School of Land and Environment. It was funded 50/50 between the City of Melbourne and Melbourne Water.

The key design considerations were that the maximum weight loading available was 100 kg per square metre. The roof had a pitch of 1:100, and there was limited access for maintenance and construction. Minimal or no irrigation was required.

A decision was taken to create a sedum roof which would incorporate some experimental planting of various Australian native plants. The main planting comprised *Sedum pachyphyllum*, *Oscularia deltoides*, *Sedum reflexum*, *Sedum mexicanum*, *X Sedaveria* cv. The Australian plants were *Crassula sieberiana*, *Disphyma crassifolium*,

Calandrinia eremea, Leptorhynchos spp, Rutidosis leptorhynchoides and *Swainsonia formosa.* The raised circles were planted up with *Cotyledon orbiculata, Senecio mandraliscae, Crassula falcata, Aloe aries, Kalanchoe tormentosa.*

A mix of Bayswater sand, filter and coir compost was created for growing mix. Planting was undertaken on a grid-like pattern across the main roof area with soil depths of 85 to 150mm (3.5 to 6in). There were also a series of raised planting circles of 200mm (8in) depth.

The concept has worked well and has been popular with the users of the Venny.

TORONTO CITY HALL, CANADA

In 2010, a green roof was installed on the second storey Podium building above Nathan Philips Square, part of the Toronto City Hall complex. The roof cost $2.2 million to complete and now attracts thousands of visitors. Covering 37,000 ft^2, it is the largest living roof in Toronto.

The retrofit design posed major problems. Workers were subject to time restrictions because the City Hall and Square stayed open. When council sessions were in progress, construction work had to stop. In addition, all construction had to work around the timetable of scheduled events organized within the square. There were also technical challenges posed by aesthetic and historic requirements. Soon after construction of the green roof began, it was discovered that the existing roof had been built without a slope – contrary to the information given to the designers. The slope had originally existed, but had been removed during a previous renovation. As a result, the drainage facilities and insulation thickness had to be redesigned taking the level of the paving higher. This made it a building code issue. An existing guardrail built around the perimeter of the podium had to be heightened, which in turn led to heritage and cost implications.

It took forty-four days just to get the plants onto the roof. This task was separate from the need to take down the old interlocking stone and insulation and bringing all the new materials. As people were working in the building, the contractors had to close off a street to get the materials onto the Podium – and the square could only be used for this task when there were no people present. Materials were frequently unloaded and loaded at 5am when the building was empty.

Public safety caused further problems. As the Podium could not be sealed off, contractors had to watch for curiosity seekers walking up the outdoor ramp from the square below. A scaffold roof had to be constructed to protect people going into the building at the back.

When City Hall was originally built, there were few high-rise buildings nearby. Modern development has led to the creation of many high-rise buildings in the neighbourhood, creating a wind tunnel effect. Often the workforce on the Podium project would arrive on site to discover that all the work that had been completed the previous day had been blown around, and had to be replaced. All the drainage boards had to be continuously weighted down.

The eventual design comprises a paved courtyard, a deck café and a mosaic garden with benches. All the plants came in a pre-vegetated tray system. Linear plantings comprising sedums, perennials and grasses are arranged in a palette of purple, pink, yellow/orange, and green as visitors circle the City Hall's two towers. Shade structures over the public benches act as sundials. According to designer Mary Tremain, 'Only at certain times of the day does the sun cast a shadow on each bench. There's a two o'clock shade bench, a twelve o'clock shade bench and a morning bench.'

The edge of the Podium roof is lined with a walkway paved with planks interlocking with the flower beds. The courtyard is lit with light columns while the mosaic garden is illuminated by lights recessed into the roof edge guardrail, creating the effect of a glowing garden when seen from adjoining buildings.

VANCOUVER CONVENTION CENTER, CANADA

In 2008 the Vancouver Convention Center underwent a major expansion tripling its total

The green roof above the Vancouver Convention Center. (Photo: PWL/DA Architects & Planners)

Aerial view of the Vancouver Convention Center in its waterside setting. (Photo: VCC PWL Partnership)

size. The aim was to create a totally sustainable building possessing a 6.5 acre green roof. This project made it the largest non-industrial green roof in North America and the largest green roof in Canada.

The building design helped shape the decision for the roof and the type of roof. The architects describe the building as a 'landform' building and as such a green roof was felt to be ideal for this site. The design team looked at a number of options for the landscape roof overlay and decided that a coastal grassland model was preferable. This type of landscape naturally occurs in the area, and is able to withstand high drought as well as very wet conditions. The habitat is aesthetically pleasing and easy to maintain.

The roof is an unusual design as it sets out to imitate a gulf island beachfront and provides a nesting ground for local birds on slopes ranging from 3 per cent to 56 per cent inclines. To achieve this, the roof was constructed using several layers. The initial layer comprises a fibreglass mat panel with a gypsum core on top of a metal roof base. Over this the designers placed a capillary waterproofing material that includes a root inhibitor, followed by 10cm (4in) of extruded insulation covered with a filter cloth. The final layer is a customized growth medium made of sand (5–7 per cent) and organic matter (15–25 per cent). This mix is diluted with lava rock (55–70 per cent) to create the overall mix. The weight of the roof is 39.6lb per square foot when fully saturated. There is no peat moss as the designers preferred not to use this ecological resource. The sand comes from dredging of the shipping channels in the local Fraser River while the organic matter comprises composted wood and garden waste. In total over 5,000m^3 of growing medium weighing over 11 million pounds was used.

Because of the extreme slopes to be found in some parts of the roof, additional web-style retention systems were incorporated. These were made from high-strength polymer matting and stainless steel cables to hold the growing media, plants and 43Km of drip irrigation piping in place. The roof is kept watered by a mix of natural rainwater and grey water systems. Drainage and water recovery systems collect and disperse rainwater through the roof using the drip-feed piping controlled by eight moisture sensors placed strategically throughout the roof. In addition, the building's grey water treatment process collects and cleans water from toilets for use in the irrigation system during summer whenever the moisture content of the growing medium falls below 15 per cent of the fully saturated level.

400,000 indigenous plants and grasses from the Gulf islands were planted on the roof so as to create a natural habitat for local wildlife. The plant list comprises:

Plugs

- Common thrift (*Armeria maritima*)
- Douglas aster (*Aster subspicatus*)
- Slimstem reed grass (*Calamagrostis stricta*)
- Dense sedge (*Carex densa*)
- Chamiso sedge (*Carex pachystachya*)
- Pacific meadow sedge (*Carex pansa*)
- Berkeley sedge (*Carex tumulicola*)
- Beach strawberry (*Fragaria chiloensis*)
- 'Pacifica' silverweed (*Potentilla anserine*)
- Broad-leafed stonecrop (*Sedum spathulifolium*)

Seed

- Bent grass (*Agrostis pallens*)
- Pearly everlast (*Anaphalis margaritacea*)
- California poppy (*Eschscholzia maritime*)
- Idaho fescue (*Festuca idahoensis*)
- 'Quatro' sheep's fescue (*Festuca ovina vulgaris*)
- Creeping red fescue (*Festuca rubra*)
- June grass (*Koeleria macranthe*)
- California blue-eyed grass (*Sisyrinchium bellum*)

Bulbs

- Hooker's onion (*Allium acuminatum*)
- Nodding onion (*Allium cernuum*)
- Harvest brodiaea (*Brodiaea coronaria*)
- Fool's onion (*Brodiaea hyancinthina*)
- Common camas (*Camassia quamash*)

No chemical fertilizers, pesticides or herbicides are used on the roof. Each year, the roof is 'mowed' in the autumn and clippings are composted back into the soil as fertilizer.

The roof acts as a natural habitat for birds, insects and small mammals. During its first summer, house sparrows were seen on the roof rooting around the grass seedheads. It is also home to four beehives providing honeybees to pollinate the flowering plants. A screen has been installed to protect the hives from the prevailing winds.

Linking into the green roof is an artificial reef. This has been designed into the foundations of the building and provides a habitat for barnacles, mussels, seaweed, starfish, crabs and fish. In total it provides 200ft of shoreline and 1,500ft of marine habitat. The five-tier structure has been constructed from 76 concrete frames weighing more than 36,000Kg each.

It is anticipated that the roof will reduce summer heat gains by up to 95 per cent and winter heat losses by up to 26 per cent.

The roof has proved very hardwearing. It has already experienced two winters and, because all the plants are native to the region, has coped well with the wet weather. The plant ecology is perfect for the maritime location and extremes of long hot dry summers followed by cool wet winters.

The complex has been designed by Seattle-based LMV Architects in collaboration with Vancouver-based Musson Cattell Mackey Partnership, DA Architects & Planners and landscape architects PWL Partnership.

Bruce Hemstock of PWL Partnership said:

> Our biggest issue during the design phase was the selection of plant species and logistics of including plant species that are not commercially grown. We worked closely with the native plant nursery to ensure that wild seed collection, conditioning and testing was carried out and that the viability of the plant and seed could be relied upon for the project.

Preparing for the construction of the green roof on a Celebrity Cruise ship. (Photo: Jorg Breuning/Green Roof Services LLC)

ABOVE: Preparing the surface. (Photo: Jorg Breuning/Green Roof Services LLC)

BELOW: Laying the green roof. (Photo: Jorg Breuning/Green Roof Services LLC)

ABOVE: **Laying out the turf. (Photo: Jorg Breuning/Green Roof Services LLC)**

BELOW: **Overview of the Lawn Club. (Photo: Jorg Breuning/Green Roof Services LLC)**

We were also keenly aware of the volumes of rainwater that would need to be dealt with in a roof of this size. The development of a drainage and collection strategy that used standard roof drains was a key part of the design process. The zigzag pattern you see on the roof are roof runnels that mimic a stream and actually break up the roof into discreet drainage areas.

ROYAL CARIBBEAN CRUISE LINERS

Mobile green roofs have been installed on several Royal Caribbean cruise ships that travel around the Mediterranean, Northern Atlantic and Caribbean. The roofs were installed by Jorge Breuning of Green Roof Service LLC.

The first ship, *Celebrity Solstice*, had a 15,000 ft^2 green roof installed in 2008. Installation took place at Meyer Werft in Germany. The green roof is situated on the top deck of the ship and is known as the Lawn Club. It provides a facility for guests to relax and play lawn games. Dan Hanrahan, President and CEO of Celebrity Cruises, said:

> We want our guests to experience the unexpected, like the thrill of sinking a putt on a freshly manicured lawn in the middle of the ocean.

Before installation, considerable testing took place in Miami and Germany as well as on a cruise ship so as to decide which type of grass would be most suited to the site. The design specifications were considerable:

- The green roof had to be able to cope with Arctic, Northern European, Mediterranean and Caribbean weather.
- Wind resistance was essential as the roof would experience winds of up to 100mph and gusts of over 120mph.
- There was a maximum weight of 130 metric tons.
- The grass was required to be salt tolerant.
- The grass had to be high quality turf able to support games such as croquet and golf putting.
- The actual roof structure had to be sufficiently stable to withstand sliding – the ship tilts up to 12 degrees or 27 per cent.

Apart from its aesthetic and amenity qualities, the roof also has in-built sustainability with a water run-off collection tank.

The roof has proved popular and successful. Other green roofs have been installed on other ships within the fleet, namely *Celebrity Equinox*, *Celebrity Eclipse* and *Celebrity Silhouette*.

In August 2010, Jorg Breuning commented:

> The *Solstice* is now two years old and we changed the entire grass once after the first 120,000 guests. The grass ages fast but we have been able to keep it thriving in all climate zones. The ships are cruising for about one year before it needs to be replaced. Most football and soccer stadiums change their grass two to four times a year with probably 10 per cent of the traffic we have. So we are very happy with our design and our experience paid off. Heavy storms with nearly 40ft waves and wind speeds of over 100 mph caused some minor salt issues in a few sections on one ship. We are able to replace our proprietary pre-grown grass mixture in Florida and in Rome, Italy. More locations (Asia) might come in two years. The entire set-up will last as long as the ships' lifetime – thirty years.

Celebrity Solstice received the Green Roofs for Healthy Cities 2009 Awards of Excellence as a Special Recognition which stated 'although impressive on its own, the Lawn Club stands out all the more for being part of a ship-design philosophy concerned with overall sustainability including elements such as photovoltaics, reuse and refining of oil on board and a water run-off collection tank for the green roof itself.'

SANDS SKY PARK, SINGAPORE

The Sands Sky Park sits on top of the three hotel towers at Marina Bay Sands, Singapore. This 1.2 hectare tropical oasis is longer than the Eiffel Tower is tall and large enough to park four and a

The swimming pool and trees high above adjacent buildings. (Photo: Marina Bay Sands)

Public observation deck at Sands Sky Park. (Photo: Marina Bay Sands)

half A380 jumbo jets. It extends to form one of the world's largest public cantilevers.

The Sky Park is part of the $5.5 billion Marina Bay Sands development owned by Las Vegas Sands Corporation. The development includes hotels, shopping mall, convention centre, restaurants, casinos, nightclubs, theatres and a museum which will feature international exhibitions.

Construction work on the Sands Sky Park started in 2009 and it was opened to the public on June 24 2010. The Sky Park superstructure weighs over 7,000 tonnes and is made up of fourteen individual parts, which were lifted using a unique combination of bridge and building technology, making it among the highest strand-jacking operations ever undertaken.

The Sands Sky Park is situated 200m in the sky, and rests across the three hotel towers. It contains:

- exclusive restaurants including The Sky on 57
- a spectacular public observation deck that can host hundreds of people
- a 159m infinity swimming pool, the world's largest outdoor pool at that height
- 12,400m^2 of space
- landscaped gardens that are home to 250 trees and 650 plants.

The landscaped gardens are reminiscent of gardens at ground-floor level. Planting focuses the use of native plants.

Trees growing on the Sands Sky Park comprise:

- Black olive (*Bucida buceras*)
- Black rosewood, East Indian rosewood (*Dalbergia latifolia*)
- Red coral tree (*Erythrina glauca*)
- Red water tree, sassy bark (*Erythrophleum guineense*)
- Bebaru, sea hibiscus (*Hibiscus tiliaceus 'purpureum'*)
- Penang sloe (*Kopsia flavida*)
- Crepe myrtle, rose of India (*Lagerstroemia speciosa*)
- Frangipani (*Plumeria rubra*)
- Crepe jasmine (*Tabernaemontana divaricata*)
- Keruntum (*Tristania obovata*).

Palms used on the Sands Sky Park comprise:

- Betel nut (*Areca catechu*)
- Bentinck palm (*Bentinckia nicobarica*)
- Foxtail palm (*Wodyetia bifurcate*)
- Macarthur palm (*Ptychosperma macarthurii*).

Members of the public can access the cantilever, which is the largest outdoor observation deck at that height. This observation deck is ticketed for non-hotel guests. The three swimming pools are only available to hotel guests.

AUGUSTENBORG BOTANICAL ROOF GARDEN, MALMO, SWEDEN

Founded in 2001, the Augustenborg Botanical Roof Garden was the world's first botanical garden on a roof. Located in the city of Malmo, Sweden; it was designed as both a demonstration area and a research garden testing plants, engineered soils, stormwater run-off and establishment methods. The Swedish Agricultural University is responsible for all the research testing that is undertaken in the garden.

The garden comprises a mix of extensive and intensive gardens spread across several industrial buildings joined by footbridges and occupies a total of 102,258ft^2. One of the buildings involved is the Scandinavian Green Roof Institute. The pitch of the gardens varies from roof to roof, with some being flat, others at a pitch of up to 4 degrees. There are regular guided tours for groups, and the gardens are accessible by wheelchair. One of the largest roofs contains five inspiration gardens:

- **Climbing garden** – soil layer averages 15 to 20cm (6 to 8in) with soil built up in mounds around bamboo sticks supporting climbers like Virginia Creeper. Sedum provides ground cover.
- **Hilly landscape** – these are small hills made of polystyrene and covered with grass mats

and dry grassland flower species. The hills are up to 1.6m high.

- **Decking and containers** – this area has a wooden floor surrounded by lavender hedges. There are wooden containers for flowers and herbs, as well as a series of connected ponds.
- **Water garden** – this comprises a stream of water flowing down a slate riverbed with water vegetation and meadow flowers. The soil level is up to 15cm (6in) deep. Polytyrene was used to create the shape of the valley.
- **Gravel plot** – this is a biodiverse roof. Substrate was taken from different locations in Malmo in which rare plants, native to industrial sites and railways in the city, are grown. Seeds are collected from the roof plants and returned to suitable sites around the city for planting. The roof garden provides a habitat for native species, as well as invertebrates and birds such as the black redstart. Gravel depths range from 10 to 15cms (4 to 6in).

Other roofs within the Botanical Roof Garden include extensive sedum roofs, and a solar powered roof in which sedum is grown in wave-like shapes.

Construction of the Botanical Roof Garden took three years and it now provides the city of Malmo with a major tourist attraction. The Roof Garden forms part of a larger project called Ecocity Augustenborg, which is designed to regenerate buildings from the 1950s and 1960s by incorporating green facilities such as renewable energy and stormwater management.

AMERICAN SOCIETY OF LANDSCAPE ARCHITECTS (ASLA), WASHINGTON, USA

A decision was taken to retrofit an area of roof on the ASLA headquarters building as a green roof in 2004. The eventual scheme took two years to complete. The aim was to provide educational, viewing and recreational opportunities. Landscape architects Michael Van Valkenburgh Associates Inc were commissioned to undertake the project. An existing stairway was extended to provide access for viewing and using the roof.

Creating a green roof on the existing problem raised questions of weight loading. The 3,000ft^2 roof includes a lift shaft. As a result the soil depths and plantings were varied across the roof so as to take advantage of differing load capacities. The elevator shaft was found to be strong enough to take 21in of soil enabling planting in that area to include sumac trees which can grow up to 30ft when mature.

The aim was to make the green roof feel like a garden. At the same time it would also be a laboratory trialling species, apart from sedums, that could thrive in shallow soil and under the harsh environmental conditions typical of US urban rooftops. The final design includes both native and introduced plant species. Flowering perennials such as goldenrod, spiderwort, black-eyed Susan, artemesia, butterfly milkweed, blue gamma grass and Virginia wild rye were included.

The design features two separate elevated 'Waves' facing each other with each wave rising to a height of 8ft. The North Wave contains a 15cm (6in) deep semi-intensive system containing native and non-native flowering herbaceous perennials and grasses. The South Wave incorporates a shallower 10cm (4in) deep substrata suitable for an extensive system which is planted with sedum. A central viewing platform enables plants to be seen at eye level. A lightweight, aluminium grating set 3in above the terrace allows sedum to be seen blooming at the feet of visitors from another extensive green roof system underneath. Although the sedum may get trampled a bit where they poke through the grating, they will survive. The grating maximizes the planting area as well as providing walkable space on the roof.

The Waves are created out of Styrofoam and act as noise insulators from the air conditioning units. During construction, strong winds threatened to tear the foam from its anchors while the shape and angle of the foam made the situation worse. Structural engineers developed a system where the arching steel frames of the landforms were linked by a net of steel cables anchoring the foam waves to the roof trusses below. Once secured, the waves were covered in a thin layer of soil and growing medium.

The staircase area was covered with 30cm (12in) of growing medium and planted up with sumacs, pasture rose and New Jersey tea. The lift shaft could be covered with 53cm (21in) of growing medium allowing a flame sumach and a trumpet vine covering a trellis to be grown.

The roof acts as an urban habitat for birds, pollinating insects and butterflies.

Temperature monitoring systems have been in place since the roof was completed. The green roof has been found to have a maximum temperature difference of 43.5° lower than a neighbouring black roof. A 10 per cent reduction in building energy use was reported during the winter months. Water retention levels are high. Between July 2007 to May 2007, the green roof retained nearly 75 per cent of the total rainfall.

Plant growth has varied according to location. Growth was slowest on the south mound where planting coverage was thinnest and hottest. Within the intensive garden, Ceananthus americanus (New Jersey tea) struggled, but *Rhus copallina* (flame sumach), *Rhus aromatica* (smooth sumach), *Campsis radicans* (trumpet vine) and *Rosa carolina* (pasture rose) proved very successful. Grasses survived well on the roof, as did *Allium cernuum* and *Coreopsis verticillata.*

Nancy Somerville, ASLA Executive Vice President states 'We wanted to create a space to push the envelope of green roof design, educate the public on the benefits of green roofs, provide an amenity to our staff and facilitate easy data monitoring – all within a 3,000ft^2 footprint.' The roof is now used for everything from yoga classes to public tours.

CREATIVE DISCOVERY MUSEUM, CHATTANOOGA, USA

The Creative Discovery Museum in Chattanooga, USA retrofitted a green roof. It covers over 3,000ft^2 and is planted with sedums and small trees. The green roof was manufactured by LiveRoof and installed by Engineered Verdant Solutions, a division of Stein Construction. It will become an additional habitat for butterflies, songbirds and insects including the museum's own honeybees.

Installation took only a few days. A protective membrane was installed to protect the existing roof. Modular containers made of recycled plastic held a few inches of soil and full-grown sedum plants. These containers were laid directly on top of the membrane and were connected to each other to create the roofing system. Shallow planter boxes were installed on top of the walls surrounding the roof. These planters contain a variety of annuals and perennials such as *vinca*, black-eyed Susan and *echinacea*. The aim of the planter is to enhance the views from the second-storey windows and provide extra flowers for the bees. A grid walkway was installed to provide access for maintenance.

The roof will provide a new environmental educational opportunity. 'While the public will not have direct access to the roof, there will be multiple views available on the second story and in the tower. Additional educational information will be posted explaining the benefits of green roofs and how they work,' according to the museum.

Executive director Henry Schulson says:

> The green roof is an important part of our efforts to become a more environmentally friendly institution. The green roof will not only provide environmental benefits to the museum and the community, it will also be viewed by thousands of children and families every year who will learn the many ways that a green roof can help create a better planet.

FORD TRUCK ASSEMBLY PLANT, DEARBORN, MICHIGAN, USA

In 2004, the Guinness Book of World Records highlighted the world's largest green roof as being the 454,000ft^2 (4.1 hectare) space on top of the Ford Truck assembly plant at Dearborn,

Michigan. The green roof is regarded as an important part of the site's stormwater management system. It forms part of the company's visitor education programme highlighting environmentally beneficial site and building strategies.

The design specifications required that the floor had to be deliberately lightweight so as to cope with the 50ft (15.25m) structural spans. Availability of plant material was a major consideration. Orders were placed a year in advance of installation so as to ensure that enough material could be cultivated. *Sedum* 'Fulda glow' and '*diffusum*' were chosen and pre-planted onto blankets prior to installation. The growing medium was one inch deep and consisted of 7–9mm of porous stone, sand, and organic material. A mineral wool fleece material to absorb rainwater was added, together with a geotextile mesh. The vegetation was cut into 3.28×6.56ft, palletized and transported to the site by crane. The green roof has a total saturated weight of 10lb per square foot. An irrigation system was installed to help the plants acclimatize to the roof setting.

Ford anticipates that the green roof will retain 447,000 gallons of rainwater annually, approximately 50 per cent of the overall amount experienced each year. The green roof is linked into a series of swales and wetland ponds which allow the surplus rainwater to be treated naturally before returning to the river. This was seen as a way of avoiding having to install a water treatment facility. Improvement of the habitat overall was another reason for installing the green roof since it would attract wildlife, primarily birds and insects, to an area which previously had no vegetation. An apiary was established on the visitor centre site adjacent to the Truck Assembly Plant.

HIGH LINE PARK, NEW YORK, USA

This has been described as the 'longest green roof in the world'. Located in New York, it has been created out of former railway tracks which ran high above the city streets. The New York High Line was created in 1930 aiming to remove railways from on the city streets to above them. The new railway tracks were built on stilts ranging from 5 to 9m high and 9 to 18m wide. The route covered 2.5km from the Convention Center and Gansevoort Street. It closed in 1980. For the next twenty years, vegetation grew naturally on the tracks until a group of property owners sought to have it demolished. A 'Friends of the High Line' was set up to fight the demolition proposals. The Friends gained a lot of support – over 10,000 people signed up, many of them celebrities, and were able to overturn the demo-lition order signed by Mayor Rudy Giuliani.

By December 2002 the High Line was placed under a preservation order and plans were being laid to create a high level garden. Landscape architect James Corner, architects Diller Scofidio and horticultural expert Piet Oudolf won the competition to design the project. The resultant park has been an overwhelming success. Access to the High Line is via stairs and lifts and it is cared for by the city of New York. It can be used only during the day time.

The tracks remain visible so as to maintain the historical authenticity of the project. Pathways, ponds and benches were added, and planting consists of 210 plant species including bushes and trees which grow on 45cm (18in) of substrate. The park is confined by the limits of the High Line – wide enough for two trains to pass each other. Over 2,000,000 people have now visited the park, enjoying spectacular views of the Empire State Building, the Hudson River and the Statue of Liberty.

TARGET CENTER, MINNESOTA, USA

In 2009, a green roof was installed on the Target Center, Minnesota. This is a basketball arena, home to the NBA Minnesota Timberwolves and the WNBA Minnesota Lynx. It also acts as the main concert and event venue in Minnesota – for example it has hosted Metallica, *American Idol*, Rod Stewart, Beyonce and President

Aerial view of the green roof above the Target Center Minnesota, USA. (Design team: Kestrel Design Group, Inspect and Leo A Daly; photo: Bergerson Photography)

Obama. Nathalie Hallyn of the Target Center comments:

> The decision to re-roof as a green roof was informed by a lifecycle cost comparison we performed which showed that over the lifetime of the green roof, the green roof was slightly more economical than a traditional roof. The primary challenge in the design and construction of this green roof was the limited structural capacity as maximum green roof saturated weight was restricted to 17.4 lbs per square foot.

This weight limit is less than is customary for green roof projects but increasing the structural capacity on the roof was prohibitive. The project went ahead by reducing the amount of growing medium available. This in turn limits the water-holding capacity available for the plants. To compensate for this, a very lightweight, engineered growing medium was used together with a water retention fabric designed to withstand constant dampness, high alkalinity as well as varying hydrostatic pressures. Over 11 miles of drip irrigation systems with piping situated every 18in plus moisture sensors to maximize irrigation efficiency were installed. To test for leaks and enable any leaks in the future to be accurately pinpointed, an Electric Field Vector Mapping® leak detection system was installed.

The green roof consists of a 7cm (2.75in) deep growing area located in the centre of the main arena plus a deeper 9cm (3.5in) growing area around the perimeter where the structural capacity is greater so as to maximize the growing medium available for plant growth. The scheme also required 14,000 cement pavers being laid to provide firebreaks as well as roof protection. Recycling played an important part in the construction of the roof. The design team set out to recycle most of the old roof into the new project, using in an estimated 450tons of existing rock, 590tons of existing pavers, 140tons of existing roofing membrane and over sixty truckloads of existing roof insulation being reused.

The plant palette was limited to species that are extremely tolerant of drought and shallow soil profile and started with a pre-vegetated mat to give the plants a head start.

The roof was planted with twelve species of

sedums and twenty-two species of prairie plants native to Minnesota. Green roof designer the Kestrel Design Group used a mix of seeds, plugs, pre-grown mats and on-site cuttings. Plant varieties included *Sedum album* 'Coral carpet', *Sedum sexangulare, Sedum alacondium, Sedum spurium* 'Dragon's blood', *Sedum middendorffianum diffusum, Sedum hybridum* 'Immergrünchen', *Allium canadense, Anemone patens, Antennaria neglecta, Aster ericoides, Geum triforum, Liatris punctata, Viola pedata, Lupinus perennis, Aster ptarmicoides, Dalea purpurea, Solidago nemoralis.* Seed mixes included *Allium stellatum, Asclepias verticillata, Cassia fasciculata, Liatris aspera, Coreopsis palmate* and *Penstemon grandiflorus.* The lupins were deliberately planted to encourage the kamer blue butterfly, an endangered species that needs lupins to survive.

The roof is the largest green roof in Minnesota and the first North American arena to incorporate such a facility. The construction contract included a twenty-year green roof warranty as well as a twenty-year maintenance contract for both the waterproofing and the vegetated components of the roof. Nathalie Hallyn explains:

> At 113,000ft^2, the Target Center green roof mitigates the urban heat island effect, greens views from above, provides wildlife habitat and improves urban air quality on a scale that is not feasible at grade in an urban area like downtown Minneapolis. It also mitigates stormwater run-off from a significant amount of impervious surface in a downtown location where space does not permit use of other low impact development techniques for stormwater management.

SOLDIER FIELD, CHICAGO USA

Soldier Field is one of the biggest projects to take place in Chicago since the impetus to green the city began. Soldier Field is home to the Chicago Bears stadium, which originally opened in 1926 and was designed as a monument to the veterans of the First World War. As part of the redevelopment plans, the new stadium restored the historic exterior and colonnades and also the parkland setting. 17 acres of additional public waterfront parkland was obtained from former parking areas and garages. The rooftop area element of the park covers 5.5 acres on top of a sloping garage roof. It is bisected by a plaza, which is converted to a pedestrian facility on event days. The main aim of the rooftop park is to blur the edges of the parking garage so that it blends into the surrounding park which is full of maples, oaks, hawthorns, ash and lindens. The edges of the garage were bulked up using 45ft of foam concrete, creating deeper growing areas for tree planting which would enclose the roof lawn on three sides.

To one side of the entrance to the parking facilities, hawthorns were planted on the roof in a radiating grid pattern. Soil depths across the roof range from 15cm (6in) at the sloping turf areas to 75cm (30in) where trees are planted. Burning bush and winter creeper were planted as groundcover together with fine fescue as a low-maintenance turf grass.

Creation of the green roof was not easy, as the weight of the garage could not support much construction equipment. As a result, all the materials including growing mediums were taken to the roof and moved along using conveyors. The roof has a 2.5 per cent pitch.

Soil systems were designed to store surface water for use by the vegetation. The roof deck itself has a growing medium which allows percolation rates of between 6in and 15in per hour. When maximum capacity is reached, the water moves into the aggregate drainage layer and by using the slope of the deck moves into a traditional clay drainage pipe cut into the structural foam. Volumetric water sensors are used to control irrigation on critical slopes.

The roof and surrounding parkland is very popular, attracting thousands of visitors each year.

8 THE FUTURE

The concept of green roofs has already gone a significant way with greater attention being paid to the use of native plants rather than international varieties. Alongside this there are indications of a move away from passive to active use of roofs.

The passive use of a green roof is now well established. People are accustomed to considering the energy savings, environmental considerations and stormwater run-off. What is now happening is that attention has begun to switch to investigating ways in which roofs can be actively used by incorporating solar panels into the green roof and encouraging the development of energy. Roofs are being seen as an integral part of the overall sustainability of a building. Then there is the question of how a green roof can be used for farming or the production of crops by restaurants; as well as increasing the level of amenity use by local communities.

Considerable interest is also being shown in the potential for using roofs as food growing areas. It is a logical progression. As the world's cities expand, so demand for fresh produce increases. Energy costs mean that there is a demand for food miles to be kept as low as possible. Urban farming is seen as a new source of food with green roof techniques being used to grow food on balconies and roofs. Given the number of flat roofs that exist in every city above apartment blocks, offices and factories; this could provide acres of potentially valuable farming space. The United States and Canada are very much in the forefront of this movement. Urban farming is taking over the idea of people just growing a few vegetables on balconies and roofs. Rooftop farming is expanding into large-scale operations growing crops of wheat, kale, chard, potatoes, strawberries, Jerusalem artichokes and rhubarb to name but some of the many crops. US Professor Dickson Despommier of New York's Columbia University has taken the concept a step further and developed the idea of a skyscraper farm in which buildings are devoted to growing fruit and vegetables. He believes that multi-storey buildings could be designed as giant hothouses to grow food and recycle water from roofs. The installation of large solar panels could provide clean, renewable energy.

OPPOSITE: A bio-diverse roof at Regents Place, London, designed to provide a variety of wildlife habitats. (Photo: Alumasc)

Entrepreneurs have recognized the opportunity for new business initiatives.

In New York City, a rooftop farm scheme known as the Brooklyn Grange project has been set up. It covers just 1 acre of rooftop. According to their web page on Kickstarter.com, this is:

> a project that requires a lot of hard work and one that sets an example for using under-utilized rooftop space across this dense city to do something productive. We plan to use a simple green roof infrastructure to install over 1 million lbs of soil on the roof of an industrial building on which vegetables will be grown nine months of the year. The aim is that the farm will create a new system of providing local communities with access to fresh, seasonal produce. We plan to expand quickly in the first few years, covering multiple areas of New York City's unused rooftops with vegetables. The business has many environmental and community benefits, and allows our city

Basil growing in a rooftop farm in America. (Photo: Sky Vegetables)

> dwelling customers to know their farmer, learn where their food comes from, and become involved.

The farm is open to the public and is located on an industrial roof in Long Island, Queens. The roof was protected by the installation of root protection and waterproofing membranes before having 1 million lbs of soil placed on the roof by crane.

On a much wider scale, Bright Farm Systems and Sky Vegetables are combining to use hydroponics (growing vegetables without soil) to create commercial scale farms on urban rooftops. Bob Fireman, president of Sky Vegetables claims 'we can grow twenty times the amount of food using less than 5 per cent of the water used by conventional soil based farming.' Bright Farm/Sky Vegetables believe that its systems could help building owners save even more money on their heating costs. The Bright Farm/Sky Vegetables concept is designed for commercial and residential roofs of at least 10,000ft^2 and incorporates solar panels to heat greenhouses where the plants grow in water. The greenhouses lower building costs by absorbing sunlight in the summer and providing additional insulation in the winter. Bright Farms would rent the roofs, thus ensuring that the building owners gain an extra income stream from hitherto unused roof space. The aim is to create food which would take only forty-eight hours to go from farm to table. 'We're talking to subsidized housing groups and public buildings where fresh lettuce can go into a cafeteria and people can take home fresh vegetables,' says Bob Fireman.

John Domino of Sky Vegetables does add a caveat to this.

> We do not have a maximum roof height. However, we do require use of a freight elevator and access to a ground-floor loading dock and are looking at greenhouses that are 20,000–40,000ft^2 or more in size. Therefore I think that most skyscrapers are probably not a good fit. In general I see us going on buildings that are one to five storeys high. However, especially on new buildings, I think we can be designed to work with most building heights. The roofs need to accommodate two means of stairway access for fire safety and also a freight elevator to move products and supplies to and from the greenhouse.

He adds:

> our incremental roof loads are pretty small, especially in areas where there is a significant (30–40lb per square foot) snow load. There may be some strengthening needed in those locations and there may also be a need to provide some additional lateral bracing to handle the increased wind loading on the building. The greenhouses are very sturdy structures and are designed to cope with high winds and heavy rains. Our basic plan is to capture the rainwater that hits our greenhouse roof and reuse that to feed our plants. The key to being able to perform the rainwater capture is to have an area 30x40in for a 40,000ft^2 greenhouse to place rainwater storage tanks.

Over in Michigan, USA, manufacturer Trenton Forging has created its own rooftop greenhouse so as to process unused energy from its own manufacturing processes. It has designed a system that harnesses heat from the forging operation that would otherwise be wasted. Trenton Forging is using the energy to heat water to fuel a greenhouse located on top of the company's industrial plant. The forge heats metal to temperatures between 1,600° and 1,800°. After they are formed, the metal pieces are placed into big bins and set outside to cool. Bins are rolled under a 4,000 gallon tank inside the plant which heats water to warm the greenhouse. Forced air and hot water heaters are used to keep the greenhouse warm in winter. It is proving very successful, raising a harvest of lettuce, spinach, kitchen herbs, tomatoes and flowers.

Attention is also beginning to focus on the way in which roofs can be used for honey bees. One of the first rooftop gardens designed specifically for honey bees was installed on the American Ice Company Building in Baltimore. Designed by Jorg Breuning, Green Roof Service LLC and Architecture & Design Inc; the 5,500ft^2 roof features an ever-blooming array of plants and a water source for the bees. The roof is planted up with sedum matting plus a semi-intensive area with large patches of densely planted perennials and shrubs ideal for honey bees: *Panicum varigatum* 'Northwind', *Calamagrostis acutiflora* 'Karl Forester', *Buddleia davidii* 'Nanho', *Viburnum pragense*, *Muscari armeniacum*, *Opuntia basilaris*, *Sedum spurnum*, *Sedum album*, *Juniperus chinensis* 'Spartan', *Agastache rupestris*, *Aster laevis* 'Bluebird', *Boltonia aster* 'Snowbank', *Delosperma cooperi*, *Echium russicum*, *Nepeta x faassenii* 'Walker Low', *Lavendula* a. 'Provence', *Origanum*, *Thymus*, Crocus, Daffodils, Narcissus, *Caryopteris* 'Longwood blue', *Perovskia a.* 'Superba', *Solidago* 'Fireworks', *Calamintha* 'White Cloud'.

In Canada, the roof of the Fairmont Hotel, Vancouver provides $40,000 worth of herbs a year for use by the chefs working in its kitchens. In British Columbia, the Canada Church St Wine Bar uses its roof to grow herbs in milk crates lined with rubbish bags. It also grows tomatoes, chilli peppers, strawberries, edible calendula and nasturtium flowers. The main challenge has not been the weather conditions or the location but raccoons that have been eating the chilli pepper plants. It also houses a honey bee apiary with nearly 500,000 resident honey bees. Chefs use the produce to make culinary delights such as honey ganache chocolates.

The Ecological Garden at Linnaea Farm, Cortes in British Columbia grows radishes, dandelion, chard, beets, nettles, arugula, carrots, beans, cucumbers, tomatoes, nasturtiums and herbs on the roof. The plants are grown in ice cream buckets and bins filled with soil. The major difficulties have been the need to ensure that the roof joists can take the weight of 1,200ft^2 of waterlogged soil and regular human access. Access too can be a problem, as researchers have found that coming down a ladder with backpacks full of produce is not always easy.

Montreal saw its first rooftop farm being set up in 2010. Located on a two-storey office building near Marche Centrale, Montreal; the 31,000ft^2 greenhouse has been installed by Lufa farms. Co-founder Kurt Lynn aims to use the farm to shorten the distance between the people who grow food and the people who buy it, commenting that in Quebec some produce on sale in supermarkets travels more than 1,500Km after being harvested. By setting up a rooftop greenhouse, Lynn believes it will be possible to grow fresher, more fragile and better tasting varieties.

Ultimately, rooftops open up untold potential for rooftop growing. Nick Buck of Drivers Jonas has even suggested that roofs could be used for growing short rotation coppice as a biofuel!

Linking walls and roofs is another possibility. Having made the step of recognizing the energy and environmental advantages of growing on roofs, it is not a large step to looking at the walls supporting the roofs. For centuries, there have been plants such as ivy and Virginia creeper growing against walls, encouraging wildlife and providing an additional layer of insulation. Living walls can reduce the external temperature of a building from between 10°C and 60°C to 5°C and 30°C. Other benefits include helping to create oases of greenery within an urban area, and to reduce noise, pollution and heat island effects. They create visual interest and obscure unsightly features. There are indications that green walls can help biodiversity by linking the wall with a green roof as it can create corridors for migratory species. In the USA, the National Wildlife Federation is developing a programme to create corridors of habitat using native plant growth.

Now, people are looking at ways of developing the green wall concept. Vertical walls are being developed which are supported by a framework away from the wall, or are walls with plants growing in them. The concept was introduced as an experiment by Patrick Blanc, a French botanist looking at ways of creating a garden without dirt. He studied tropical rainforest plants and developed a system for growing them on walls lined with felt as a way of bringing greenery into cities. He says, 'When you live in towns, you don't always go into gardens. It's really important to use empty spaces to invite nature into town.' His living walls are now used on commercial and institutional buildings world wide, including the Athenaeum Hotel and the Musée du Quai Branly in Paris.

Different variations on living wall construction are already emerging. There are the traditional green facades using self-clinging plants like ivy or plants supported on walls using wires. This has been adapted with the development of trellis and cable/wire rope net systems that support plants while keeping them slightly away from a wall thus making maintenance easier. Living Walls comprise pre-vegetated panels, modules or planted blankets fixed to a wall or frame. Plants can be put into a pouch, which is a small grow-bag. These are used to grow a wide range of plants including groundcover, ferns, shrubs, perennials and edible plants. Such walls require more intensive maintenance than a green facade. There are also landscape walls, which are sloping rather than totally vertical and made from stacking material such as plastic or concrete.

A short-term wall was set up in Copenhagen during 2010. More than 5,000 plants from all over Europe were used to create a green facade for the headquarters of the European Environment Agency (EEA). The planting was designed to mimic a map of Europe in Bloom. All the plants used were annuals. The whole design was mounted on a steel frame designed by architect Johanna Rossbach and structural engineer Peter Lund Christiansen.

Over in Canada, designers have created a 3,000ft^2 green wall at the Semiahmoo Public Library and Royal Canadian Mounted Police Facility in Surrey, British Columbia. Over 10,000 plants were used on the wall. It is a self-sufficient vertical garden attached to the exterior and interior of the building. Plants are grown using hydroponic technology, rather than conventional soil. The plants grow the vertical surface akin to the way they do on cliffs and around waterfalls. Water loss is minimized since it only occurs through transpiration and evaporation, and not as a result of leaching through the soil.

In the UK, a new Hall of Residence for the University of Liverpool will feature green roofs with wildlife habitats built into the brickwork. The design incorporates rainwater harvesting and solar thermal water heating plus an air source heat pump.

Living Walls are becoming increasingly popular on a wider scale. All-in-one kits and ready-made systems have been created. ELT, an Ontario company that began trading as a green roof supplier, moved into selling living wall systems in 2007. It is now one of the biggest suppliers of the systems in North America. According to company president Greg Gardner, green wall sales have increased 300 per cent since 2008. In 2010, the company began introducing a cheaper lighter kit designed for home gardeners with prices starting at about $40 per one square foot panel. Walls now account for 80 per cent of the company's business.

Another US company, Green Living Technologies, make green walls using a proprietary system of panels. The panels are made from recyclable aluminium or stainless steel and can be completely vertical set against the walls of a building. The panels are deep enough to support grass and even vegetables to be grown while still allowing airflow and water flow between it and the building walls. One of their flagship projects is on the Pittsburgh PNC building, which has the largest green wall in North America. The 2,400ft^2 wall contains over 15,000 ferns, sedums and other plants. PNC, the owners of the building, believe it will help insulation as well as being decorative since it is estimated that the office

Looking to the future – new growth on a green roof at Acorn Close allotments, Levenshulme, Manchester. (Photo: Little Green Roofs, Manchester)

space behind the wall will be about 25 per cent cooler during the summer.

In Monterrey, a house has been built which has green walls and a green roof. The green wall covers 2,691ft^2 and was installed in August 2009 using BioPared modules made of recycled polyethylene. The modules were planted on site so that the drought-loving plants could adapt more easily to the summer conditions. In August, temperatures were around 110°F (43°C) and similar temperatures continued for a further two months. Eight plants were used per module giving a total of 8,000 plants overall.

Irrigation is required for this type of wall gardening. Modular systems filled with soil generally incorporate a sprinkler or drip irrigation system. A waterproof barrier is often added to protect the walls.

Three main problems have emerged among advocates of living walls. It is important to ensure that the walls get enough light and that they are strong enough to bear the structures. Above all, irrigation is important and has to be well maintained. Living walls do require much more maintenance than a conventional wall, or green roof.

And what of transport? Sedum has been used to cover a car, albeit in an artistic fashion! While in America, the Bus Roots movement has resulted in the creation of the BioBus. Although the practicality of the project is uncertain, the concept is certainly thought provoking. BioBus is the idea of

An early version of the BioBus with small sedum roof at the rear. (Photo: Marc de Castro)

How a sedum roof fits into a BioBus. (Photo: Marc de Castro)

Marc Castro Cosio of New York and was developed as part of his university studies. His idea is to create mobile green roofs on top of buses. He comments 'if we grew a garden on the roof of every one of the 4,500 buses in the MTA bus fleet, we would have 35 acres of new rolling green space in the city.'

The MTA fleet comprises 4,500 buses, each with a roof surface area of 340ft^2. Bus Roots aims to connect citizens with their community while trying to use minimum resources and improve the environment. It seeks to reclaim forgotten spaces. The first Bus Roots green roof was installed on the BioBus in 2010. The bus has been travelling around New York City and as far as Ohio in order to promote the concept, while carrying out research on the effects of motion on plants. The roof is said to be successful and popular, keeping the bus cool while improving air quality in the city. It also provides a habitat for birds and insects.

The use of green roofs as a way of developing sustainability, rather than just studying the environment, is also developing fast. The most prominent example is Boston Latin School, which combines outdoor classrooms, greenhouses, wind turbines, solar panels and a cafeteria. All groups within the school utilize information from the roof in classes, often actually working on the roof learning to grow food or gain inspiration for creative work while science classes investigate wind speed and solar energy. As the school states, the roof has become a learning laboratory.

Solar and green roofs are becoming inextrica-

A new approach to garden design – a living wall made by putting pouches of plants together.

Solar panels and a sedum roof working together in harmony. (Photo: East of Angland Co-operative Society)

bly interlinked and can no longer be seen in isolation. In Portland, Oregon University researchers are investigating the way in which solar panels can be made more effective when linked with a green roof. During the summer time, temperatures can soar. This means that rooftop surfaces can retain so much heat that the capacity of solar panels is significantly decreased. Combining a green roof system with solar panels enables the roof to lower temperatures significantly. Research has already shown that a combination of solar panels and white reflective roofing does not work as well as solar panels and a green roof. The plants keep the roof around the solar panels cooler while the solar panels provide shade to the roof plants, adding to the cooling effect. Each part of what is being called an 'eco-roof' is being monitored for temperature range, soil moisture levels and water flow as well as photosynthetic activity. In terms of solar energy levels, the roofs are reaching about 1,232kWh – which is close to the maximum rating. Over in San Francisco, the Steinhart Aquarium/Morrison Planetarium green roof incorporates 62,000 photovoltaic cells supplying 213,000kWh of energy per year.

Green roofs cannot be seen in isolation – they are increasingly seen as an integral element within a sustainable environmental programme whether it refers to drainage, heating, heat islands or biodiversity. Environmental education facilities, such as the Eco Center in San Francisco, set out to provide an introduction for any member of the public wanting to know more about sustainable buildings, green economy, renewable energy, pollution, greenhouse gas reduction, green roofs and waste water technologies. Green buildings are very much the residential and business space of the future.

Architecturally, the style of green roofs is advancing at a rapid pace, with architects and structural engineers seeking to take advantage of the new concepts. They have recognized the potential opportunities presented by green roofs to create buildings that are distinctive, yet meet all modern requirements – sustainable, green, habitat replacement, as well as dealing with urban problems such as heat islands. The result has been spectacular. On a small scale, this can be seen at the Norfolk Wildlife Trust Visitor Centre at Cley Marshes, which sets out to maximize the environmental benefits of a green roof in an unusual fashion. The roof is carefully designed with a gradual curvature at the front and steeper curve at the back. This helps to channel the northerly winds so as to increase the effectiveness of the wind turbine on the roof. On a much grander scale, there is the Wave House in France and the stunning Sands SkyPark in Singapore in which a public park balances on top of three skyscrapers and their connecting bridges. Such designs help to maximize the use of available land space and develop new ideas about living in the air.

Garden designers have been slower on the uptake, concentrating on traditional designs and ideas rather than innovation. The opportunities to investigate the possibilities presented by green roof design, such as the effects of wind on plants, remains to be developed.

In the long term, roofs seem set to continue playing a major role in developing sustainability. Researchers are already working on the creation of new technologies including roofing materials which change colour with the temperature.

It is also likely that green roof garden tours will emerge as a popular destination among architects, landscapers as well as the general public – in much the same way as open garden schemes are already popular. Google Earth offers the opportunity to experience these gardens without having to travel.

FURTHER INFORMATION

WEBSITES

Green Roofs Today
www.greenroofstoday.co.uk
An online resource promoting green roofs in the UK. Also includes the green roof directory of manufacturers, suppliers and services.

Green Roof Centre
www.thegreenroofcentre.co.uk

www.livingroofs.org
An independent website which promotes green roofs and living roofs in the UK. The portal is supported and sponsored by green roof companies in the UK.

www.greenroofs.org
This is the website of 'Green Roofs for Healthy Cities' which promotes green roofs throughout North America as well as providing training courses. Membership is a mix of private and public companies within the industry. There are over 800 members.

www.efb-greenroof.eu
This is the European Federation of Green Roof Associations. It seeks to establish industry wide standards.

www.bauder.co.uk
This is one of the largest green roof manufacturers in the UK. Bauder is a German company with branches worldwide.

www.greenroofservice.com
US-based green roof company.

www.alumasc-exteriors.co.uk
This is the website of Alumasc, one of the leading UK green roof companies.

www.mdpi.com/journal/sensors
Stuart R Gaffin, Reza Khanbilvardi and Cynthia Rosenzweig *Development of a Green Roof Environmental Monitoring and Meteorological Network in New York City.*

www.enviromat.co.uk
This is the website of sedum mat supplier, Q Lawns. They produce a free Green Roof CD rom with a useful 'How to' section.

Green roofs for healthy cities
www.greenroofs.org

International Green Roof Association
www.igra-world.com
Information on projects, conferences, workshops and green roofing worldwide.

PUBLICATIONS

English Nature Research Report number 498: Green Roofs: their existing status and potential for conserving biodiversity in urban areas.

GONG N 2007 *Green Roofs and Bumblebees: An observation of bumblebees on green roofs* Undertaken as part of M Arch Landscape Studies, University of Sheffield.

Introduction to Green Walls Technology, Benefits and Design September 2008.

Cass G. Barns *The Sod House* (Bison Books, University of Nebraska Press.

INDEX

OTHER GARDENING BOOKS FROM CROWOOD

Blackburne-Maze, Peter *The Complete Guide to Fruit Growing*
Blackburne-Maze, Peter *The Complete Guide to Vegetable Growing*
Clark, Emma *The Art of the Islamic Garden*
Cooke, Ian *Designing Small Gardens*
Cooke, Ian *Exotic Gardening*
Cox, Freda *Garden Styles*
Cunningham, Sally *Ecological Gardening*
Dorey, Paul *Auriculas – an essential guide*
Ford, Richard *Hostas – an essential guide*
Gooch, Ruth and Jonathan *Clematis – an essential guide*
Gray, Linda *Herb Gardening*
Gregson, Sally *Ornamental Vegetable Gardening*
Gregson, Sally *Practical Propagation*
Hart, Simon *Tomatoes – a gardener's guide*
Hodge, Geoff *Pruning*
Jones, Peter *Gardening on Clay*
Larter, Jack Tuberous *Begonias – an essential guide*
Lavelle, Michael *Sustainable Gardening*
Littlewood, Michael *The Organic Gardener's Handbook*
Marder, John *Water-Efficient Gardening*
Mitchell, Michael *Alpines – an essential guide*
Nottridge, Rhoda *Wildlife Gardening*
Parsons, Roger *Sweet Peas – an essential guide*
Saunders, Bridgette *Allotment Gardening*